Brazili[an] phrasebook

Daniel Grassi
Mike Harland

New York Chicago San Francisco Lisbon London Madrid Mexico City
Milan New Delhi San Juan Seoul Singapore Sydney Toronto

ISBN 978-0-07-154612-6
MHID 0-07-154612-X

McGraw-Hill books are available at special quantity discounts to use as premiums and sales promotions, or for use in corporate training programs. For more information, please write to the Director of Special Sales, Professional Publishing, McGraw-Hill, Two Penn Plaza, New York, NY 10121-2298. Or contact your local bookstore.

Publishing Manager
Anna Stevenson

Prepress
Helen C Hucker

CONTENTS

INTRODUCTION

This brand new English-Brazilian Portuguese phrasebook from Harrap is ideal for anyone wishing to try out their foreign language skills while travelling abroad. The information is practical and clearly presented, helping you to overcome the language barrier and mix with the locals.

Each section features a list of useful words and a selection of common phrases: some of these you will read or hear, while others will help you to express yourself. The simple phonetic transcription system, specifically designed for English speakers, ensures that you will always make yourself understood.

The book also includes a mini bilingual dictionary of around 5000 words, so that more adventurous users can build on the basic structures and engage in more complex conversations.

Concise information on local culture and customs is provided, along with practical tips to save you time. After all, you're on holiday – time to relax and enjoy yourself! There is also a food and drink glossary to help you make sense of menus, and ensure that you don't miss out on any of the national or regional specialities.

Remember that any effort you make will be appreciated. So don't be shy – have a go!

ABBREVIATIONS USED IN THIS BOOK

adj	adjective	*mf*	masculine and feminine
adv	adverb	*mpl*	masculine plural
art	article	*n*	noun
f	feminine	*pl*	plural
fpl	feminine plural	*prep*	preposition
inv	invariable	*sg*	singular
m	masculine	*v*	verb

PRONUNCIATION

For every sentence written in Portuguese in this guide, you will find the pronunciation given in italics. If you follow this phonetic transcription, you will be able to make yourself understood in Portuguese. Some Portuguese sounds do not exist in English, and so we have used the following codes to transcribe them:

η   this indicates a nasal sound similar to the **ng** in "flying", "playing", "toying", "sang" (note the "g" is never pronounced): eg **mãe** *myη*, **pão** *powη*, **põe** *poyη*, **lã** *lahη*

J   similar to the **j** in the French word "je", or the **s** in "vision", eg **justo** *Joos-too*, **jogar** *Joo-gaH*

H   as in English, or the **ch** sound in the Scottish word "loch", eg **carro** *ka-Hoo*, **rato** *Hah-too*

Vowels

Most vowels in Portuguese form a long sound, especially **i** and **u** (pronounced *ee* and *oo*).

When you see **a**, **e** and **o** followed by "h" (*ah, eh, oh*), this should be pronounced with the long vowel sound (as in English "c**a**r", "p**ay**" and "s**o**").

Otherwise **a**, **e** and **o** should be pronounced with the short vowel sound (as in English "p**a**t", "p**e**t" and "p**o**t").

See the special sound η above for vowels which have nasal sounds.

Alphabet

a	*a* (as in "p**a**t")	**g**	*Jeh*	**m**	*em**ee***
b	*beh* (as in "b**ay**")	**h**	*aga* (as in "**agha**st")	**n**	*en**ee***
c	*seh*	**i**	*ee*	**o**	*o* (as in "h**o**t")
d	*deh*	**j**	*Jota*	**p**	*peh*
e	*e* (as in "p**e**t")	**k**	*kapa*	**q**	*keh*
f	*eff**ee***	**l**	*ell**ee***	**r**	*eH**ee***
s	*ess**ee***	**v**	*veh*	**y**	*eep-seelon*
t	*teh*	**w**	*dabl-yoo*	**z**	*zeh*
u	*oo*	**x**	*sheess*		

Note that the **bold** letters indicate that you should stress that syllable.

EVERYDAY CONVERSATION

Brazilians are on the whole quite informal when speaking to others and the word **você** (plural **vocês**) will fit most situations where we use "you" in English. Where we might use "sir" or "madam" for more polite situations, **o senhor** or **a senhora** can also be used in Portuguese. It is usual to shake hands when being introduced to someone, and in meetings amongst friends people often greet each other with a kiss on each cheek. A word frequently used to say "Hi!" when you meet somebody is **Oi!**, as in **Oi, Jorge, tudo bom?** – "Hi Jorge, how are things?"

The basics

bye	tchau *tchah*-oo
excuse me	desculpe *dess-kool*-pee, com licença *koŋ lee-sen-sa*
good afternoon	boa tarde *boh-a tar*-djee
good evening	boa noite *boh-a noy*-tchee
good morning	bom dia *boŋ djee-a*
goodbye	tchau *tchah*-oo
goodnight	boa noite *boh-a noy*-tchee
hello	olá *oh-lah*
hi	oi *oy*
how are things?	tudo bom? *too-doo boŋ*
maybe	talvez *tal-vess*
no	não *nouŋ*
OK	ok *oh-kay*
pardon	perdão *pair-down*, desculpe *dess-kool*-pee
please	por favor *poor fa-voH*
sorry!	desculpe! *dess-kool*-pee!
thanks, thank you	obrigado *(m)*/obrigada *(f) oh-bree-gah-doo/oh-bree-gah*-da
yes	sim *seeŋ*

Expressing yourself

I'd like ...
gostaria de ...
goss-ta-ree-a djee ...

we'd like ...
gostaríamos de ...
goss-ta-ree-a-mooss djee ...

do you want ...?
quer ...?
kair ...?

do you have ...?
você tem *(sg)*/vocês têm *(pl)* ...?
vo-seh tayŋ/vo-sehss tay-ayŋ ...?

is there a ...?
há um *(m)*/uma *(f)* ...?
ah oom/oo-ma ...?

are there any ...?
há algum *(m)*/alguma (f) ...?
ah al-goom/al-goo-ma ...?

how ...?/how?
como é que ...?/como?
koh-moo eh keh ...?/koh-moo?

why ...?/why?
por que é que ...?/por quê?
poor-keh eh keh ...?/poor-keh?

when ...?
quando ...?
kwan-doo ...?

what ...?/what?
o que é que ...?/o quê?
oo keh eh keh ...?/oo keh?

where is ...?
onde fica...?
on-djee fee-ka ...?

where are ...?
onde ficam ...?
on-djee fee-kowŋ ...?

how much is it?
quanto custa?
kwan-too kooss-ta?

what is it?
o que foi?
oo keh foy?

do you speak English?
você fala inglês?
vo-seh fah-la een-glehss?

where are the toilets?
onde fica o toalete?
on-djee fee-ka oo twa-leh-tchee?

how are you?
como você está?
koh-moo vo-seh eess-ta?

fine, thanks
bem, obrigado *(m)*/obrigada (f)
bayŋ, oh-bree-gah-doo/oh-bree-gah-da

thanks very much
muito obrigado *(m)*/obrigada (f)
mweeŋ-too oh-bree-gah-doo/oh-bree-gah-da

no, thanks
não, obrigado *(m)*/obrigada (f)
nowŋ, oh-bree-gah-doo/oh-bree-gah-da

yes, please
sim, por favor
seen, poor fa-voH

you're welcome
de nada
djee nah-da

see you soon
até mais
a-teh ma-eess

see you later
até logo
a-teh lo-goo

I'm sorry
desculpe
dess-kool-pee

Understanding

aberto	open
atenção	attention
cuidado	attention
entrada	entrance
entrada livre/grátis	free entry
fechado	closed
fora de serviço	out of order
grátis/gratuito/de graça	(for) free
homens (H)	gents
não incomodar	do not disturb
ocupado	busy/occupied
perigo	danger
proibido ...	do not ...
proibido fumar	no smoking
quebrado	out of order
reservado	reserved
saída	exit
sanitários	toilets
senhoras (S)	ladies
vago	free/vacant
WC	toilets

há ...
there is/there are ...

bem-vindo/vinda
welcome

você se importa se ...?
do you mind if ... ?

um momento, por favor
one moment, please

PROBLEMS UNDERSTANDING PORTUGUESE

Expressing yourself

pardon?
perdão?
pair-down ?

what?
o quê?
oo keh?

could you repeat that, please?
poderia repetir?
po-deh-ree-a Heh-peh-tcheeH?

could you speak more slowly?
poderia falar mais devagar?
po-deh-ree-a fa-laH ma-eess djee-va-gaH?

I don't understand
não entendo
nown en-ten-doo

I understand a little Portuguese
entendo um pouco de português
en-ten-doo oom poh-koo djee por-too-gehss

I can understand Portuguese but I can't speak it
entendo português, mas não falo
en-ten-doo por-too-gehss, mass nown fah-loo

I hardly speak any Portuguese
meu português é muito limitado
meh-oo por-too-gehss eh mween-too lee-mee-tah-doo

how do you say … in Portuguese?
como é que se diz … em português?
koh-moo eh keh see djeess … ayn por-too-gehss?

how do you spell it?
como é que se escreve?
koh-moo eh keh see eess-kreh-vee?

what's that called in Portuguese?
como é que se chama em português?
koh-moo eh keh see shah-ma ayn por-too-gehss?

could you write it down for me?
você poderia escrever?
vo-seh po-deh-ree-a eess-kreh-veH?

Understanding

entende português?
do you understand Portuguese?

significa ...
it means ...

(deixe que) eu escrevo
I'll write it down for you

é um tipo de ...
it's a kind of ...

SPEAKING ABOUT THE LANGUAGE

Expressing yourself

I learned a few words from my phrasebook
aprendi algumas palavras com a ajuda do meu guia de conversação
a-pren-djee al-goo-mass pa-lah-vrass koŋ ah a-Joo-da doo meh-oo ghee-a djee kon-ver-sa-sowŋ

I studied Portuguese for a while but I've forgotten everything
estudei português por algum tempo mas já esqueci tudo
eess-too-day por-too-gehss poor al-goom tayŋ-poo mass Jah eess-kess-ee too-doo

I can just about get by
sei me virar
say mee vee-raH

I hardly know two words!
não sei quase nada!
nowŋ say kwah-zee nah-da!

I find Portuguese a difficult language
acho português muito difícil
ah-shoo por-too-gehss mween-too djee-fee-seew

I know the basics but no more than that
sei algumas coisas básicas, mas não mais do que isso
say al-goo-mass koy-zass bah-zee-kass, mass nowŋ ma-eess doo keh ee-soo

people speak too quickly for me
as pessoas falam muito rápido
ass peh-soh-ass fah-lowŋ mween-too Ha-pee-doo

Understanding

você tem uma boa pronúncia
you have a good accent

você fala muito bem português
you speak very good Portuguese

ASKING THE WAY

Expressing yourself

excuse me, can you tell me where the ... is, please?
desculpe, pode me dizer onde fica ...?
dess-kool-pee, po-djee mee djee-zair on-djee fee-ka ...?

which way is it to ...?
qual é o caminho para ...?
kwal eh oo ka-meen-yoo pah-ra ...?

can you tell me how to get to ...?
poderia me dizer como eu chego a ...?
po-deh-ree-a mee djee-zair koh-moo eh-oo sheh-goo ah ...?

is there a ... near here?
tem ... aqui perto?
tayŋ ... a-kee pair-too?

could you show me on the map?
poderia me dizer onde fica no mapa?
po-deh-ree-a mee djee-zair on-djee fee-ka noo mah-pa?

is it far/near?
é muito longe/perto?
eh mween-too lon-Jee/pair-too?

I'm looking for ...
estou procurando ...
eess-toh proh-koo-ran-doo ...

I'm lost
estou perdido *(m)*/perdida *(f)*
eess-toh pair-djee-doo/pair-djee-da

Understanding

à direita   right
à esquerda   left

descer	to go down
seguir	to follow
continuar indo	to keep going
reto em frente	straight ahead
subir	to go up
virar	to turn
dar a volta	to turn back

você está a pé ou de carro?
are you on foot or do you have a car?

são cinco minutos de carro/a pé
it's five minutes by car/on foot

é a primeira/segunda rua à esquerda
it's the first/second street on the left

vire à direita na rotatória
turn right at the roundabout

vire à esquerda no semáforo
turn left at the traffic lights

siga reto em frente
go straight ahead

saia na próxima saída
take the next exit

é pertinho/não fica longe
it's quite close/it's not far

é bastante longe
it's quite far

é só virar a esquina
it's just round the corner

GETTING TO KNOW PEOPLE

The basics

bad	ruim *Hoo-eeŋ*
beautiful	lindo/linda *leen-doo/leen-da*
boring	chato/chata *shah-too/shah-ta*
cheap	barato/barata *ba-rah-too/ba-rah-ta*
expensive	caro/cara *kah-roo/kah-ra*
good	bom/boa *boŋ/boh-a*
great	espetacular *eess-peh-ta-koo-laH*
interesting	interessante *een-teh-reh-san-tchee*
not bad	nada mal *nah-da mahw*
pretty	bonito/bonita *boh-nee-too/boh-nee-ta*
ugly	feio/feia *fay-oo/fay-a*
(very) well	(muito) bem *(mweeŋ-too) bayŋ*
to hate	detestar *deh-tess-taH*
to like	gostar (de) *goss-taH (djee)*
to love	adorar *a-doh-raH*

INTRODUCING YOURSELF AND FINDING OUT ABOUT OTHER PEOPLE

Expressing yourself

my name's ...
meu nome é ...
meh-oo no-mee eh ...

how do you do!
como você está?
ko-moo vo-seh eess-ta?

what's your name?
como você se chama?
ko-moo vo-seh see shah-ma?

pleased to meet you!
muito prazer!
mweeŋ-too pra-zeH!

this is my husband
este é o meu marido esta é
ehss-tchee eh oo meh-oo ma-ree-doo

this is my partner, Karen
a minha companheira, Karen
ess-ta eh a meen-ya kom-pan-yay-ra, karen

I'm English
sou inglês (m)/inglesa (f)
soh een-glehss/een-gleh-za

we're American
somos americanos (m)/americanas (f)
soh-mooz ah-meh-ree-kah-nooss/ah-meh-ree-kah-nass

I'm from ...
sou de ...
soh djee ...

where are you from?
de onde você é?
djee on-djee vo-seh eh?

how old are you?
quantos anos você tem?
kwan-tooz ah-nooss vo-seh tayɳ?

I'm 22
tenho 22 anos
ten-yoo veen-tchee ee doyss ah-nooss

what do you do for a living?
o que é que você faz?
oo keh eh keh vo-seh fass?

are you a student?
você é estudante?
vo-seh eh eess-too-dan-tchee?

I work
eu trabalho
eh-oo tra-bal-yoo

I'm studying law
estou estudando Direito
eess-toh eess-too-dan-doo djee-ray-too

I'm a teacher
sou professor (m)/professora (f)
soh pro-fess-oH/pro-fess-or-a

I stay at home with the children
trabalho em casa e tomo conta das crianças
tra-bal-yoo ayɳ kah-za ee toh-moo kon-ta dass kree-an-sass

I work part-time
trabalho em meio turno
tra-bal-yoo ayɳ may-oo toor-noo

I work in marketing
trabalho em marketing
tra-bal-yoo ayɳ marketing

GETTING TO
KNOW PEOPLE

I'm retired
sou aposentado/aposentada
soh a-poh-zen-tah-dooa-poh-zen-tah-da

I'm self-employed
trabalho por conta própria
tra-bal-yoo poor kon-ta pro-pree-a

I have two children
tenho dois filhos
ten-yoo doyss feel-yooss

we don't have any children
não temos filhos
nowŋ teh-mooss feel-yooss

two boys and a girl
dois meninos e uma menina
doyss meh-nee-nooss ee oo-ma meh-nee-na

a boy of five and a girl of two
um menino de cinco anos e uma menina de dois anos
oom meh-nee-noo djee seen-koo ah-nooz ee oo-ma meh-nee-na djee doyss ah-nooss

have you ever been to Britain?
você conhece a Grã-Bretanha?
vo-seh kon-yess-ee a graŋ breh-tan-ya

GETTING TO KNOW PEOPLE

Understanding

você é inglês/inglesa?
are you English?

também estamos de férias
we're also on holiday

conheço bem a Inglaterra
I know England quite well

eu adoraria ir à Escócia um dia
I'd love to go to Scotland one day

TALKING ABOUT YOUR STAY

Expressing yourself

I'm here on business
estou aqui a negócios
eess-toh a-kee ah neh-goss-yooss

we're on holiday
estamos de férias
eess-tah-mooss djee feh-ree-ass

I arrived three days ago
cheguei há três dias
*sheh-**gay** ah trehss **djee**-ass na*

we've been here for a week
chegamos faz uma semana
*sheh-**gah**-mooss fass **oo**-ma seh-**mah**-*

I'm only here for a long weekend
vou ficar aqui apenas um fim de semana
*voh fee-**kar** a-**kee** a-**peh**-nass oom feeŋ djee seh-**mah**-na*

we're just passing through
estamos só de passagem prolongada
*eess-**tah**-mooss so djee pa-**sah**-Jayŋ pro-lon-**gah**-da*

this is our first time in Brazil
é a primeira vez que visitamos o Brasil
*eh ah pree-**may**-ra vess keh vee-zee-**tah**-mooss oo bra-**zeew***

we're on our honeymoon
estamos em lua-de-mel
*eess-**tah**-mooss ayŋ **loo**-a djee mehw*

we're here with friends
estamos com uns amigos
*eess-**tah**-mooss koŋ oonz a-**mee**-gooss*

we're touring around the north-east
estamos visitando o Nordeste
*eess-t**ah**-mooss vee-zee-**tan**-doo oo nor-**dess**-tchee*

we managed to get a cheap flight
conseguimos um vôo barato
*kon-seh-**ghee**-mooss oom **voh**-oo ba-**rah**-too*

we're thinking about buying a house here
estamos pensando em comprar uma casa aqui
*eess-**tah**-mooss pen-**san**-doo ayŋ kom-**prar** oo-ma **kah**-za a-**kee***

Understanding

boa estadia!
enjoy your stay!

bom resto de férias!
enjoy the rest of your holiday!

é a primeira vez que você visita o Brasil?
is this your first time in Brazil?

quanto tempo vai ficar?
how long are you staying?

está gostando?
do you like it here?

você já foi a …?
have you been to …?

STAYING IN TOUCH

Expressing yourself

we should stay in touch
vamos nos manter em contato
vah-mooss nooss man-tair ayŋ kon-ta-too?

here's my address, if ever you come to Britain
este é o meu endereço, se um dia resolver visitar a Grã-Bretanha
*ehss-tchee eh oo **meh**-oo en-deh-**reh**-soo, see oom **djee**-a He-zol-**veH** vee-zee-**tar** a graŋ breh-**tan**-ya*

Understanding

você me daria o seu endereço?
will you give me your address?

você tem (endereço de) e-mail?
do you have an e-mail address?

se quiser nos visitar, será muito bem-vindo/a
you're always welcome to come and stay with us here

EXPRESSING YOUR OPINION

Some informal expressions

é incrível it's amazing
foi divertidíssimo it was loads of fun
foi muito divertido it was great fun
foi um pouco chato it was a bit boring

17

Expressing yourself

I really like …
gosto muito de …
goss-too mweeη-too djee …

I really liked …
gostei bastante de …
goss-tay bass-tan-tchee djee …

I don't like …
não gosto de …
nowη goss-too djee …

I didn't like …
não gostei de …
nowη goss-tay djee …

I love …
adoro …
a-doh-roo …

I loved …
adorei …
a-doh-ray …

I would like …
gostaria de …
goss-ta-ree-a djee …

I would have liked …
eu teria gostado de …
eh-oo teh-ree-a goss-tah-doo djee …

I find it …
acho …
ah-shoo …

I found it …
achei …
a-shay …

it's lovely
é uma maravilha
eh oo-ma ma-ra-veel-ya

it was lovely
foi uma maravilha
foy oo-ma ma-ra-veel-ya

I agree
concordo
kon-kor-doo

I don't agree
não concordo
nowη kon-kor-doo

I don't know
não sei
nowη say

I don't mind
não me importo
nowη mee eem-por-too

I don't like the sound of it
não me agrada muito
nowη mee a-grah-da mweeη-too

it sounds interesting
parece interessante
pa-ress-ee een-teh-ress-an-tchee

it was boring
foi chato
foy shah-too

it really annoys me
me irrita profundamente
mee ee-Hee-ta pro-foon-da-men-tchee

it's a rip-off
é uma roubalheira
eh oo-ma Hoh-bal-yay-ra

it gets very busy at night
à noite tem muita animação
ah noy-tchee tayŋ mween-ta a-nee-ma-sowŋ

it's too busy
tem muita gente
tayŋ mween-ta Jen-tchee

it's very quiet
é muito tranqüilo
eh mween-too tran-kwee-loo

I really enjoyed myself
me diverti muito
mee djee-vair-tchee mween-too

we had a great time
a gente se divertiu muito
a Jen-tchee see djee-vair-tchee-oo mween-too

there was a really good atmosphere
o ambiente era excelente
oo am-bee-en-tchee eh-ra eh-seh-len-tchee

we met some nice people
conhecemos pessoas muito simpáticas
kon-yess-eh-mooss pess-oh-ass mween-too seem-pa-tchee-kass

we found a great hotel
encontramos um hotel excelente
en-kon-trah-mooz oom oh-tew eh-seh-len-tchee

Understanding

gosta de ...?
do you like ...?

se divertiram?
did you enjoy yourselves?

você devia ir a ...
you should go to ...

recomendo ...
I recommend ...

é uma região muito bonita
it's a lovely area

não há muitos turistas
there aren't too many tourists

não vão no fim de semana, há muita gente
don't go at the weekend, it's too busy

não é tão bom como dizem
it's a bit overrated

TALKING ABOUT THE WEATHER

Some informal expressions

chove muito it's pouring down
está um frio de rachar it's freezing
hoje está um calor de matar today is a real scorcher

Expressing yourself

what is the weather forecast for tomorrow?
qual é a previsão do tempo para amanhã?
kwal eh a preh-vee-zown doo tem-poo pah-ra a-man-yan?

it's going to be nice
vai estar bom
va-ee eess-taH bon

it isn't going to be nice
não vai estar muito bom
nown va-ee eess-taH mween-too bon

it's really hot
está muito calor
eess-tah mween-too ka-loH

it rained a few times
choveu algumas vezes
sho-veh-oo al-goo-mass veh-zeess

it gets cold at night
à noite esfria bastante
ah noy-tchee eess-free-a bass-tahn-tchee

the weather was beautiful
o tempo esteve uma maravilha
oo tem-poo eess-teh-vee oo-ma ma-ra-veel-ya

there was a thunderstorm
teve um temporal
teh-vee oom tem-por-ahw

it's been lovely all week
o tempo esteve muito bom toda a semana
oo tem-poo eess-teh-vee mween-too bon toh-da ah seh-mah-na

it's very humid here
o tempo aqui é muito úmido
oo tem-poo a-kee eh mween-too oo-mee-doo

we've been lucky with the weather
tivemos sorte com o tempo
*tchee-**veh**-mooss **sor**-tchee koŋ oo **tem**-poo*

Understanding

parece que vai chover
it looks as if it's going to rain

a previsão é de tempo bom para o resto da semana
they've forecast good weather for the rest of the week

amanhã vai fazer calor de novo
it will be hot again tomorrow

TRAVELLING

The basics

airport	aeroporto *a-air-oh-por-too*
aisle seat	poltrona no corredor *pol-troh-na noo koh-Heh-doH*
baggage claim	retirada de bagagem *Heh-tchee-rah-da djee ba-gah-Jayŋ*
boarding	embarque *ayŋ-bar-kee*
boarding card	cartão de embarque *kar-towŋ djee ayŋ-bar-kee*
boat	barco *bar-koo*
bus	ônibus *oh-nee-booss*
bus station	(estação) rodoviária *(eess-ta-sowŋ) Hoh-doh-vee-ar-ya*
bus stop	parada de ônibus *pa-rah-da djee oh-nee-booss*
car	carro *ka-Hoo*, automóvel *ow-toh-moh-vew*
coach	(bus) ônibus *oh-nee-booss*
ferry	balsa *bal-sa*
flight	vôo *voh-oo*
gate	portão (de embarque) *por-towŋ (djee ayŋ-bar-kee)*
left-luggage (office)	depósito de bagagem *deh-po-zee-too djee ba-gah-Jayŋ*
luggage	bagagem *ba-gah-Jayŋ*
map	mapa *mah-pa*
motorway	auto-estrada *ow-toh-eess-trah-da*
passport	passaporte *pass-a-por-tchee*
plane	avião *a-vee-owŋ*
platform	plataforma *pla-ta-for-ma*
return (ticket)	passagem de ida e volta *pass-ah-Jayŋ djee ee-da ee vol-ta*
road	estrada *eess-trah-da*
shuttle bus	navete *na-veh-tchee*
single (ticket)	passagem só de ida *pass-ah-Jayŋ so djee ee-da*
station	estação *eess-ta-sowŋ*

street	rua *Hoo-a*
streetmap	mapa das ruas *mah-pa dass Hoo-ass*
taxi	táxi *tak-see*
terminal	terminal *tair-mee-now*
ticket	passagem *pass-ah-Jayn*
ticket office	bilheteria *beel-yeh-teh-ree-a*
timetable	horário *oh-rar-yoo*
town centre	centro da cidade *sen-troo da see-dah-djee*
train	trem *trayn*
underground	metrô *meh-troh*
underground station	estação de metrô *eess-ta-sown djee meh-troh*
to book	reservar *Hez-air-vaH*
to check in	fazer check-in *fa-zair oo sheh-keen*
to hire	alugar *a-loo-gaH*

Expressing yourself

where can I buy tickets for ...?
onde posso comprar passagens para ...?
on-djee poss-oo kom-praH pass-ah-Jenss pah-ra ...?

a ticket to ..., please
uma passagem para ..., por favor
oo-ma pass-ah-jayn pah-ra ..., poor fa-voH

I'd like to book a ticket
gostaria de reservar uma passagem
goss-ta-ree-a djee Hez-air-var oo-ma pass-ah-jayn

how much is a ticket to ...?
quanto custa uma passagem para ...?
kwan-too kooss-ta oo-ma pass-ah-jayn pah-ra ...?

are there any concessions for students?
há desconto para estudantes?
ah djeess-kon-too pah-ra eess-too-dan-tcheess?

could I have a timetable, please?
eu poderia ver os horários, por favor?
eh-oo poh-deh-ree-a vair ooz oh-rar-yooss, poor fa-voH?

is there an earlier/later one?
há algum *(m)*/alguma *(f)* mais cedo/mais tarde?
ah al-goom/al-goo-ma ma-eess seh-doo/ma-eess tar-djee?

how long does the journey take?
quanto tempo demora (a viagem)?
kwan-too tayŋ-poo deh-moh-ra (a vee-ah-jayŋ)?

is this seat free?
(este lugar) está vago/livre?
(ehss-tchee loo-gaH) eess-ta vah-goo/lee-vree?

I think this is my seat
acho que este é o meu lugar
ah-shoo keh ehss-tchee eh oo meh-oo loo-gaH

sorry, there's someone sitting here
desculpe, está ocupado
dess-kool-pee, eess-ta oh-koo-pah-doo

could I open/close the window?
posso abrir/fechar a janela?
poss-oo a-breer/feh-shar a Ja-neh-la?

Understanding

atrasado	delayed
cancelado	cancelled
chegadas	arrivals
entrada	entrance
entrada proibida	no entry
fumantes	smoking
informações	information
não fumantes	non-smoking
partidas	departures
passagens	tickets
saída	exit
WC	toilets
WC Homens	gents
WC Senhoras	ladies

BY PLANE

The Brazilian airline TAM now operates flights with the UK instead of VARIG. There are also many European operators such as BA, Air France, TAP, IBERIA, Alitalia, etc with frequent flights to Rio, São Paulo and the north-east, especially from Heathrow. The number of flights available, and the cost, vary according to the time of year (sometimes more expensive at Carnaval time and during the summer). On arrival, SET (Secretaria de Esportes e Turismo) offers helpful state tourist information desks at the airports (daily 7.30am-10.30pm). For information before flying, see the national tourist website: **www.turismo.gov.br**

Within Brazil there are frequent shuttle services between the big cities. TAM and GOL are the main airlines, but there are also budget airlines such as BRA, Webjet and Oceanair. Flying is very popular, so you may be advised to book in advance. Children under two years old go free and those between two and twelve pay half-fare. When waiting for a flight, check for your flight **number** on the departure board, since the destination given is only the final one and in-between stops may not be shown.

Expressing yourself

where's the TAM check-in desk?
onde fica o check-in da TAM?
on-djee fee-ka oo shek-een da tam?

I've got an e-ticket
tenho uma passagem eletrônica
ten-yoo oo-ma pass-ah-Jayŋ ee-leh-troh-nee-ka

one suitcase and one piece of hand luggage
uma mala e uma bolsa de mão
oo-ma mah-la ee oo-ma bol-sa djee mowŋ

what time do we board?
a que horas é o embarque?
ah keh oh-rass eh oo ayŋ-bar-kee?

I'd like to confirm my return flight
gostaria de confirmar o meu vôo de volta
*goss-ta-**ree**-a djee kon-feer-**mar** oo meh-oo **voh**-oo djee **vol**-ta*

one of my suitcases is missing
está faltando uma mala minha
*eess-**ta** fal-**tan**-doo oo-ma **mah**-la **meen**-ya*

my luggage hasn't arrived
a minha bagagem não chegou
*a **meen**-ya ba-**gah**-Jayŋ nowŋ sheh-**goh***

the plane was two hours late
o avião chegou com duas horas de atraso
*oo a-vee-**owŋ** sheh-**goh** koŋ **doo**-ass **oh**-rass djee a-**trah**-zoo*

I've missed my connection
perdi a conexão
*pair-**djee** a koh-nek-**sowŋ***

I've left something on the plane
deixei uma coisa no avião
*day-**shay** oo-ma **koy**-za noo a-vee-**owŋ***

I want to report the loss of my luggage
gostaria de informar a perda da minha bagagem
*goss-ta-**ree**-a djee een-for-**mar** a **pair**-da da **meen**-ya ba-**gah**-Jayŋ*

Understanding

alfândega	customs
balcão de despacho de bagagem	luggage check-in counter
classe econômica	economy class
classe executiva	business class
controle de passaportes	passport control
controle de segurança	security check
embarque imediato	immediate boarding
itens a declarar (caminho vermelho)	goods to declare
nada a declarar (caminho verde)	nothing to declare

passageiro freqüente frequent flyer
retirada da bagagem luggage reclaim
sala de embarque departure lounge
vôos domésticos domestic flights

favor aguardar na sala de embarque
please wait in the departure lounge

você gostaria de um lugar na janela ou no corredor?
would you like a window seat or an aisle seat?

quanta bagagem você tem?
how many bags do you have?

foi você que fez as suas malas?
did you pack all your bags yourself?

alguém lhe pediu para transportar alguma coisa?
has anyone given you anything to take onboard?

a bagagem tem um excesso de cinco quilos
your luggage is five kilos overweight

aqui está o seu cartão de embarque
here's your boarding card

o embarque é à(s) ...
boarding will begin at ...

favor dirigir-se ao portão número ...
please proceed to gate number ...

última chamada para ...
this is the final call for ...

você pode ligar para este número para saber se a sua bagagem chegou
you can call this number to check that your luggage has arrived

BY BUS, COACH, UNDERGROUND, TRAM

The rail system in Brazil is largely used for cargo and very slow, so people tend to use buses to get around. Taxis can be quicker and much safer, especially at night. The two largest cities, São Paulo and Rio, have underground systems, although the Rio one is limited to the northern half of the city. These **Metrô** systems are very clean and by far the most comfortable way of getting around these sprawling cities. As for the old trams, the only remaining tram line now, unfortunately, is the **bondinho** in Rio linking Santa Teresa with the downtown area.

On buses and the underground a flat fare is usually charged, or else the prices are regulated – either way, it can be the cheapest way to travel. They may not be as safe as taxis, so take care to look after your valuables, just as you would in any large city.

If you are planning to do a lot of travelling around Brazil, then you will probably be best to fly the longer distances separating north and south. However, if you are hopping from city to city, there are excellent coach lines running between them – look for the nearest **Rodoviária** (coach station). Coaches are very comfortable, often air-conditioned, and you have time to enjoy the scenery. A **direto** will take you non-stop, whereas a **ping-pinga** will be much slower, stopping off in between. For long-distance night journeys look for a **semileito** or **leito** which have reclining seats.

Expressing yourself

can I have a map of the underground, please?
você poderia me dar um mapa do metrô, por favor?
*vo-**seh** poh-deh-**ree**-a mee dar oom **mah**-pa doo meh-**troh**, poor fa-**voH**?*

what time is the next bus to …?
a que horas é o próximo ônibus para …?
*a keh **oh**-rass eh oo **pross**-ee-moo **oh**-nee-booss **pah**-ra …?*

what time is the last train?
a que horas é o último ônibus?
*a keh **oh**-rass eh oo **oo**-tchee-moo **oh**-nee-booss?*

which platform is it for …?
de que plataforma parte o trem para …?
deh keh pla-ta-for-ma par-tchee oo trayŋ pah-ra …?

where can I catch a bus to …?
onde posso pegar um ônibus para …?
on-djee poss-oo peh-gar oom oh-nee-booss pah-ra …?

which line do I take to get to …?
qual é a companhia para …?
kwal eh a kom-pan-yee-a pah-ra …?

is this the stop for …?
é esta a parada para …?
eh ess-ta a pa-rah-da pah-ra …?

is this where the coach leaves for …?
é daqui que sai o ônibus para …?
eh da-kee keh sa-ee oo oh-nee-booss pah-ra …?

can you tell me when I need to get off?
você poderia me avisar onde eu devo sair?
po-deh-ree-a mee a-vee-zar on-djee eh-oo deh-voo sa-eeH?

which station is this?
que estação é esta?
keh eess-ta-sowŋ eh ess-ta?

I've missed my bus
perdi meu ônibus
pair-djee oo meh-oo oh-nee-booss

where are the lockers?
onde são os armários?
on-djee sowŋ ooz ar-mar-yooss?

where is left-luggage?
onde é o depósito de bagagem?
on-djee eh oo deh-po-zee-too djee ba-gah-Jayŋ?

Understanding

acesso ao trem	to the trains
bilhete metrô/balsa	tube and ferry combined ticket *(in Rio)*

bilhete metrô/ônibus	tube and bus combined ticket
bilhete simples	single ticket
bilheteria	ticket office
dias úteis/sábados/domingos e feriados	weekdays/Saturdays/Sundays and holidays
longo percurso	long distance
lugar reservado	reserved seats only
meia passagem	student ticket
múltiplo 10	book of ten tickets *(Rio)*
múltiplo 12	book of twelve tickets *(SP)*
navete	airport shuttle
passagens para o próprio dia	tickets for travel today
pré-pago	pre-paid
primeira classe	first class
reservas	bookings
segunda classe	second class
tarifa de bordo	on-board ticket

há uma parada um pouco mais à frente à direita
there's a stop a bit further along on the right

você precisa trocar em …
you'll have to change at …

você precisa pegar o ônibus número …
you need to get the number … bus

este trem pára nas estações de …
this train calls at …

são mais duas paradas
two stops from here

sem serviço aos sábados e domingos
no service Saturdays and Sundays

apenas às sextas-feiras
Fridays only

BY CAR OR TAXI

For journeys across Brazil you might hire a car, as there are good federal motorways linking the major cities, but be warned that away from the main highways, as in most of Latin America, drivers have little road discipline and in rural areas there are often unmarked potholes and other dangers at night. In areas such as the Amazon, the roads are especially bad or non-existent and travelling by boat is your best bet here.

If you do hire a car in Brazil, you will have to be 21 years old and you should always carry with you your passport, international driving licence and car hire documentation, as well as proof of insurance. Traffic drives on the right, and the speed limits are 110kph (70mph) on national highways and 80kph (50mph) in cities. There are three types of fuel in Brazil (petrol, alcohol and gas), so you will need to check which fuel your car uses, rather than worrying about leaded, unleaded or diesel!

Even in the big cities driving can be a nerve-racking experience if you don't know your way around, so consider using public transport instead and let the experts do the hard work!

Certainly, taxis are relatively cheap. They can be recognised by their red number plates in São Paulo, while in Rio the cabs are yellow with a blue stripe. Ask your hotel to call a fixed-fare taxi, if possible, and avoid picking up unofficial cabs roaming the streets. Make sure the meter is on and check you aren't being overcharged – the tariff should be on **bandeira 1**, unless you are travelling after midnight, on Saturdays after 14.00, Sundays and public holidays, in which case **bandeira 2** will be used. Tipping is not normally necessary. At airports look for the special desks where you can pay for a fixed-fare voucher, charged according to the distance travelled, and hand this to the taxi driver.

Expressing yourself

where can I park?
onde posso estacionar?
*on-djee **poss**-oo eess-tass-yoh-**naH**?*

where can I find a service station?
onde posso encontrar uma estação de serviço?
*on-djee **poss**-oo en-kon-**trar** oo-ma eess-ta-**sowη** djee sair-vee-soo?*

how much is it per litre?
quanto custa o litro?
*kwan-too **kooss**-ta oo **lee**-troo?*

fill up the tank, please
completa, por favor
*kom-**pleh**-ta, poor fa-**voH***

we got stuck in a traffic jam
ficamos presos num engarrafamento
*fee-**kah**-mooss **preh**-zooss noom en-ga-**Hah**-fa-**men**-too*

is there a garage near here?
há alguma oficina aqui perto?
*ah al-**goo**-ma oh-fee-**see**-na a-**kee** pair-too?*

can you help us to push the car?
vocês podem nos ajudar a empurrar o carro?
*vo-**sehss** po-**dayη** nooz a-Joo-**dar** a em-poo-**Har** oo ka-Hoo?*

the engine won't start
o motor não pega
*oo moo-**toH** nowη peh-ga*

I've broken down
o carro pifou
oo ka-Hoo pee-foh

the battery's dead
a bateria está descarregada
*a ba-teh-**ree**-a eess-**ta** djeess-ka-Heh-**gah**-da*

we've run out of petrol
ficamos sem gasolina
*fee-**kah**-mooss sayη ga-zoh-**lee**-na*

I've got a puncture and my spare tyre is flat
furou o pneu e o estepe está vazio
*foo-**roh** oo **pneh**-oo ee oo eess-**tep**-ee eess-**ta** va-**zee**-oo*

I've had an accident
tive um acidente
*tchee-vee oom a-see-**den**-tchee*

I've lost my car keys
perdi as chaves do carro
*pair-djee ass **shah**-veess doo ka-Hoo*

how long will it take to repair?
quanto tempo vai levar para consertar?
*kwan-too **tem**-poo va-ee leh-**var** pah-ra kon-sair-**taH**?*

◆ Hiring a car

I'd like to hire a car for a week
eu queria alugar um carro por uma semana
eh-oo keh-ree-a a-loo-gar oom ka-Hoo poor oo-ma seh-mah-na

an automatic (car)
um carro com câmbio automático
oom ka-Hoo koŋ kam-bee-oo ow-toh-mah-tchee-koo

I'd like to take out comprehensive insurance
eu queria um seguro total
eh-oo keh-ree-a oom seh-goo-roo toh-tahw

◆ Getting a taxi

where can I get a taxi?
onde eu posso pegar um táxi?
on-djee eh-oo poss-oo peh-gar oom tak-see?

I'd like to go to ...
para ..., por favor
pah-ra ..., poor fa-voH

I'd like to book a taxi for 8pm
eu queria reservar um táxi para as oito horas (da noite)
eh-oo keh-ree-a Heh-zair-var oom tak-see pah-ra az oy-too oh-rass (da noy-tchee)

you can drop me off here, thanks
pode me deixar aqui, obrigado *(m)*/obrigada *(f)*
po-djee mee day-shar a-kee, oh-bree-gah-doo/oh-bree-gah-da

how much will it be to go to the airport?
quanto custa daqui até o aeroporto?
kwan-too kooss-ta da-kee a-teh oo a-air-oh-por-too?

◆ Hitchhiking

I'm going to...
vou para...
voh pah-ra...

can you drop me off here?
pode me deixar aqui?
po-djee mee day-shar a-kee?

could you take me as far as …?
pode me levar até …?
po-djee mee leh-*var* a-*teh* …?

thanks for the lift
obrigado *(m)*/obrigada *(f)* pela carona
oh-bree-*gah*-doo/oh-bree-*gah*-da *peh*-la ka-*roh*-na

Understanding

Some useful abbreviations

BR	federal highways
RJ	Rio state highways
SP	São Paulo state highways
BR-101	main coastal highway (4600km)
BR-116	main N-S highway
BR-230	E-W Trans-Amazonian highway

acenda os faróis	turn on your headlights
aluguel de veículos	car hire
área com parquímetro	pay and display
área de serviço	service area
desvio	diversion
devagar	slow
dirija com cuidado	drive carefully
espaços livres	spaces *(car park)*
estacionamento	car park
fim de obras	end of roadworks
fim do desvio	end of diversion
fim do perímetro urbano	end of city limits
guarde a passagem	keep your ticket
início do perímetro urbano	start of city limits
lotado	full *(car park)*
não ultrapasse pela direita	no overtaking on the right
obras a … km	roadworks … km ahead
proibido estacionar	no parking
reduza a velocidade	reduce speed
velocidade máxima permitida	max speed permitted

BY BOAT OR FERRY

Many cities along the coast of Brazil have large bays and islands, so ferry crossings are common, such as the Rio to Niterói service.
In the Amazon delta, eg the journey between Belém and Manaus, it is virtually the only reliable way to travel. Progress can be slow, so you might consider hiring a hammock (**rede**) and relaxing as you go.

Expressing yourself

how long is the crossing?
quanto tempo demora a travessia?
*kwan-too **tem**-poo deh-**moh**-ra a tra-veh-**see**-a?*

I'm seasick
estou com enjôo
*eess-**toh** koŋ en-**Joh**-oo*

Understanding

apenas pedestres	foot passengers only
passageiros com passagem válida para ...	passengers with a valid ticket for ...
primeira/última partida de ...	first/last crossing from ...
próxima partida à(s) ...	next crossing at ...
rede	hammock
temporal	bad weather
terminal da balsa	ferry terminal

Hotels are plentiful all over Brazil, even the cheaper ones being fairly clean and providing good service. In the major cities such as Rio de Janeiro and São Paulo, a deluxe hotel will still cost the same as in most other countries, ranging from £150 a night for a five-star hotel to £30 in a two-star hotel. A good guide to hotels in Brazil is the "Guia do Brasil Quatro Rodas" available from most news-stands.

Guesthouses are variously called **residência**, **casa de família** or **pensão**, and usually provide full board. A **pousada** is also a cheaper form of guesthouse or "bed and breakfast", but with extremely varying standards and without the same facilities – for example, meals other than breakfast or room service are typically not available.

Although "pousadas" will be the main type of accommodation used when visiting the smaller cities and towns around Brazil, there are other possibilities for younger people such as **albergues da juventude** (youth hostels – contact the Federação Brasileira dos Albergues da Juventude via its website: **www.hostel.org.br**), and **apartamentos** along the coastal areas. For the most basic of accommodation at rock-bottom prices you can also find **dormitórios**, but you will have to share! Also be aware that a "motel" is not exactly what it seems, since it is mainly used by couples on a short-stay basis!

Rural accommodation comes in the form of **fazendas**, which are ranches with guest facilities or **hotéis-fazendas** (farms) where you can also enjoy outdoor activities. If heading for the Amazon, try the new Eco-Hotels recently introduced to encourage ecotourism, with trips to the surrounding rainforest. These are still relatively pricy, however.

Camping should be restricted to organized sites and the Camping Clube do Brasil (**www.campingclube.com.br**) has over 50 throughout the country – people holding an "international camper's card" pay half price, which is extremely inexpensive. Service stations can be used as an alternative, unofficial way of camping, since these often have shower facilities as well as a place to eat.

The basics

bath	banheira *ban-yay-ra*
bathroom	banheiro *ban-yay-roo*
bed	cama *kah-ma*
bed and breakfast	*(place)* pousada *poh-zah-da*; *(service)* hospedagem com café da manhã *oss-peh-dah-Jayŋ koŋ ka-feh da man-yaŋ*
cable television	televisão a cabo *teh-leh-vee-zowŋ a kah-boo*
campsite	camping *kam-peeŋ*
double bed	cama de casal *kah-ma djee ka-zahw*
double room	quarto duplo *kwar-too doo-ploo*
en-suite bathroom	banheiro privativo *ban-yay-roo pree-va-tchee-voo*
family room	quarto para família *kwar-too pah-ra fa-meel-ya*
flat	apartamento *a-par-ta-men-too*
full-board	pensão completa *pen-sowŋ kom-pleh-ta*
fully inclusive	com tudo incluído *koŋ too-doo een-kloo-ee-doo*
guesthouse	pensão *pen-sowŋ*, casa de família *kah-za djee fa-meel-ya*, residência *Heh-zee-denss-ya*
half-board	meia-pensão *may-a pen-sowŋ*
hotel	hotel *oh-tehw*
key	chave *shah-vee*
rent	aluguel *a-loo-gehw*
room	quarto *kwar-too*
room with shower	quarto com chuveiro *kwar-too koŋ shoo-vay-roo*
satellite television	televisão por satélite *teh-leh-vee-zowŋ poor sa-teh-lee-tchee*
self-catering	com cozinha *koŋ koh-zeen-ya*
shower	chuveiro *shoo-vay-roo*
single bed	cama de solteiro *kah-ma djee sol-tay-roo*
single room	quarto individual *kwar-too een-djee-vee-doo-ow*
tent	barraca *ba-Hah-ka*

ACCOMMODATION

37

toilet	toalete *twa-leh-tchee*, banheiro *ban-yay-roo*
twin room	quarto duplo com duas camas *kwar-too doo-ploo koη doo-ass kah-mass*
youth hostel	albergue da juventude *al-bair-ghee da Joo-ven-too-djee*
to book	reservar *Heh-zair-vaH*
to rent	alugar *a-loo-gaH*
to reserve	reservar *Heh-zair-vaH*

Expressing yourself

I have a reservation
fiz uma reserva
feez oo-ma Heh-zair-vaë

the name's …
em nome de …
ayη noh-mee djee …

do you take credit cards?
aceita cartão de crédito?
a-say-ta kar-towη djee kreh-djee-too?

Understanding

aluga-se quarto	room for rent
cheio	full
completo	full
privado	private
quartos livres	vacancies
recepção	reception
WC	toilets

posso ver o seu passaporte?
could I see your passport, please?

poderia preencher esta ficha?
could you fill in this form?

assine aqui, por favor
sign here, please

HOTELS

Expressing yourself

do you have any vacancies?
tem quartos disponíveis?
*tayŋ **kwar**-tooss djeess-poo-**nee**-vayss?*

how much is a double room per night?
quanto custa um quarto duplo por noite?
*kwan-too **kooss**-ta oom **kwar**-too **doo**-ploo poor **noy**-tchee?*

I'd like to reserve a double room/a single room
queria reservar um quarto duplo/individual
*keh-**ree**-a Heh-zair-**var** oom **kwar**-too **doo**-ploo/een-djee-vee-doo-**ow***

for three nights
por três noites
*poor trehss **noy**-tcheess*

would it be possible to stay an extra night?
é possível ficar mais uma noite?
*eh poh-**see**-vehw fee-**kar** ma-eez oo-ma **noy**-tchee?*

do you have any rooms available for tonight?
tem quartos disponíveis para hoje?·
*tayŋ **kwar**-tooss djeess-poo-**nee**-vayss **pah**-ra oh-Jee?*

do you have any family rooms?
tem quartos para família?
*tayŋ **kwar**-tooss **pah**-ra fa-**meel**-ya?*

would it be possible to add an extra bed?
seria possível colocar uma cama extra?
*seh-**ree**-a poss-**ee**-vehw koh-loh-**kar** oo-ma **kah**-ma **ess**-tra?*

could I see the room first?
posso ver primeiro o quarto?
***poss**-oo veH pree-**may**-roo oo **kwar**-too?*

do you have anything bigger/quieter?
tem algum maior/mais silencioso?
*tayŋ al-**goom** ma-**yoH**/ma-eess see-len-see-**oh**-zoo?*

that's fine, I'll take it
está bem, fico com ele
eess-ta bayŋ, fee-koo koŋ eh-lee

could you recommend any other hotels?
você pode me indicar outro hotel?
vo-seh po-djee mee een-djee-kar oh-troo oh-tehw?

is breakfast included?
inclui café da manhã?
een-kloo-ee oo ka-feh da man-yaŋ?

what time do you serve breakfast?
a que horas é o café da manhã?
a keh oh-rass eh oo ka-feh da man-yaŋ?

where is the lift?
onde é o elevador?
on-djee eh oo eh-leh-va-doH?

is the hotel near the centre of town?
o hotel fica perto do centro?
oo oh-tehw fee-ka pair-too doo sen-troo?

what time will the room be ready?
a que horas o quarto fica pronto?
a keh oh-rass eh keh oo kwar-too fee-ka pron-too?

the key for room ..., please
a chave do quarto ..., por favor
a shah-vee doo kwar-too ..., poor fa-voH

could I have an extra blanket?
há como conseguir um cobertor extra?
ah koh-moo kon-seh-gheer oom koh-bair-tor ess-tra?

the air conditioning isn't working
o ar-condicionado não está funcionando
oo ar kon-djeess-yoh-nah-doo nowŋ eess-ta foon-see-oh-nan-doo

are there any messages for me?
há algum recado para mim?
ah al-goom Heh-kah-doo pah-ra meeŋ?

I'd like to pay now, do you accept credit cards?
eu gostaria de pagar, aceitam cartão de crédito?
*eh-oo goss-ta-**ree**-a djee pa-**gaH**, a-**say**-town kar-**town** djee **kreh**-djee-too?*

I think there's a mistake in the bill
acho que há um erro na conta
*ah-shoo keh ah oom **eh**-Hoo na **kon**-ta*

Understanding

desculpe, estamos cheios/não temos nada livre
I'm sorry, but we're full

só temos disponível um quarto individual
we only have a single room available

para quantas noites?
how many nights is it for?

como você se chama?
what's your name, please?

os quartos estão disponíveis a partir das 12h
check-in is from midday

tem de deixar o quarto (livre) antes das 11h
you have to check out before 11am

o café da manhã é servido no restaurante entre as 7h30 e as 9h
breakfast is served in the restaurant between 7.30 and 9.00

você gostaria de um jornal pela manhã?
would you like a newspaper in the morning?

o quarto ainda não está pronto
your room isn't ready yet

pode deixar a bagagem aqui
you can leave your bags here

ACCOMMODATION

YOUTH HOSTELS

Expressing yourself

do you have space for two people for tonight?
tem lugar para duas pessoas para esta noite?
tayŋ loo-gaH pah-ra doo-ass pess-oh-ass pah-ra ess-ta noy-tchee?

we've booked two beds for three nights
reservamos duas camas por três noites
Heh-zair-vah-mooss doo-ass kah-mass poor trehss noy-tcheess

could I leave my backpack at reception?
posso deixar a minha mochila na recepção?
poss-oo day-shar a meen-ya moh-shee-la na Hess-ep-sowŋ?

do you have somewhere we could leave our bikes?
há algum lugar para deixar as bicicletas?
ah al-goom loo-gaH pah-ra day-shar ass bee-see-kleh-tass?

I'll come back for it around 7 o'clock
eu venho buscar por volta das sete (horas)
eh-oo ven-yoo booss-kaH poor vol-ta dass seh-tchee (oh-rass)

there's no hot water
não tem água quente
nowŋ ah ah-gwa ken-tchee

the sink's blocked
a pia está entupida
a pee-a eess-ta en-too-pee-da

Understanding

cozinha no albergue   cooking facilities/kitchen
pátio (interior)/exterior   (covered) beer garden or patio
quarto múltiplo   dormitory
sala de convivência   common room

tem cartão de sócio?
do you have a membership card?

fornecemos lençóis
bed linen is provided

a pousada reabre às 18h
the hostel reopens at 6pm

SELF-CATERING

Expressing yourself

we're looking for somewhere to rent near town
queríamos alugar qualquer coisa perto da cidade
*keh-**ree**-a-mooss a-loo-**gaH** kwal-**keH** koy-za pair-too da see-**dah**-djee*

where do we pick up/leave the keys?
onde pegamos/deixamos as chaves?
*on-djee peh-**gah**-mooss/day-**shah**-mooss ass **shah**-veess?*

are bed linen and towels provided?
vocês fornecem lençóis e toalhas?
*vo-**sess** for-**ness**-ayη len-**soyss** ee toh-al-yass?*

is a car necessary?
precisa de carro?
*preh-**see**-za djee ka-Hoo?*

where is the pool?
onde é a piscina?
*on-djee eh a pee-**see**-na?*

is the accommodation suitable for elderly people?
o alojamento é adequado para pessoas idosas?
*oo a-loh-Ja-**men**-too eh a-deh-**kwah**-doo pah-ra pess-oh-ass ee-**doh**-zass?*

where is the nearest supermarket?
onde fica o supermercado mais perto?
*on-djee **fee**-ka oo soo-per-mair-**kah**-doo ma-eess **pair**-too?*

Understanding

favor deixar a casa limpa e arrumada
please leave the house clean and tidy after you leave

a casa está completamente mobiliada
the house is fully furnished

está tudo incluído no preço
everything is included in the price

nesta parte do país precisa de carro
you really need a car in this part of the country

CAMPING

Expressing yourself

is there a campsite near here?
há algum camping aqui perto?
ah al-goom kam-peen a-kee pair-too?

I'd like to book a space for a two-person tent for three nights
queria reservar um espaço para uma barraca dupla por três noites
*keh-ree-a Heh-zair-var oom eess-pah-soo pah-ra oo-ma ba-Hah-ka doo-pla
poor trehss noy-tcheess*

how much is it a night?
quanto custa por noite?
kwan-too kooss-ta poor noy-tchee?

where is the shower block?
onde ficam os chuveiros?
on-djee fee-kown ooss shoo-vay-rooss?

can we pay, please? we were at space ...
gostaríamos de pagar, estávamos no número ...
goss-ta-ree-a-mooss djee pa-gaH; eess-tah-va-mooss noo noo-meh-roo ...

Understanding

são ... por pessoa, por noite
it's ... per person per night

se precisar de alguma coisa, venha falar comigo
if you need anything, just come and ask

Brazil offers an immense range of cuisine, with lots of regional variations as well as foreign dishes resulting from its long history of immigration. Restaurants can be divided into the **restaurante à la carte** where you are seated and served, or the **bufê** where you can help yourself – in this case you either pay by the amount you consume, **por quilo**, or choose **bufê livre**, paying a fixed price and eating as much as you wish. There is also the very popular **rodízio**, where for a set price you can try a wonderful selection of meats accompanied with rice and beans. A traditional dish in restaurants is the **à la minuta** consisting of a steak and fried egg, accompanied by white rice, fries and salad. Service of around 10% is usually included in the bill, so tipping is not common in Brazil – if it is not included, then by all means leave something on the table.

Another favourite eating place originating in the south but now available country-wide is the **churrascaria** serving barbecued meats. Brazil's national dish is **feijoada**, a stew made of black beans, pork, sausage and pieces of dried beef, served with white rice, greens and slices of orange. On the north-east coast with its African roots, coconut, dende palm oil and seafood are the major ingredients and the food there can be extremely spicy.

For faster meals there are many self-service places of the fixed-price "rodízio" type, or cafés offering snacks, called **lanches**, with pastries such as **empadinhas** or **pastéis**. A common snack is a **misto quente**, a ham-and-cheese sandwich. Pizza is also very popular, especially in busy São Paulo where restaurants serve up endless varieties. As always you can get a hot-dog, **cachorro-quente**, and the fast food chain Bob's is nationwide. But Brazilian hot-dogs are no plain ketchup affair; they come with tomato, grated cheese, corn, peas, etc.

On the drinks side, you are again never spoiled for choice, but you must try **caipirinha**, Brazil's extremely refreshing drink, ideal for the very warm climate, made of juiced limes, sugar and of course **cachaça**, the white sugar-cane rum. This powerful spirit is often sweetened: for example try **capeta**, a cachaça mix with condensed milk, cinnamon and guarana powder. Draft beer is called **chope**, a lighter form of European lager, with brands like Brahma, Bohemia and Caracu.

For those who prefer non-alcoholic drinks, you will be in fruit-juice heaven, with small bars on every street corner! Try the Amazonian **açaí**, exotic **maracujá** (passion fruit) or **caju** (cashew – not the nut, but the vitamin C packed apple!).

The basics

beer	cerveja *sair-veh-*Ja
bill	conta *kon-*ta
black coffee	café preto *ka-feh preh-too*
bottle	garrafa *ga-Hah-fa*
bread	pão *powŋ*
breakfast	café da manhã *ka-feh da man-yaŋ*
cake	bolo *boh-loo*
coffee	café *ka-feh*
Coke®	Coca-Cola® *koh-ka koh-la*
dessert	sobremesa *soh-breh-meh-za*
dinner	jantar *Jan-taH*
espresso	cafezinho *ka-feh-zeen-yoo*
fruit juice	suco *soo-koo*
lemonade	soda limonada *soh-da lee-moh-nah-da*
lunch	almoço *al-moh-soo*
main course	prato principal *prah-too preen-see-pahw*
menu	cardápio *kar-dah-pee-oo*
mineral water	água mineral *ah-gwa mee-neh-rahw*
red wine	vinho tinto *veen-yoo tcheen-too*
rosé wine	vinho rosé *veen-yoo Hoh-zeh*
salad	salada *sa-lah-da*
sandwich	sanduíche *sand-wee-shee*
sparkling	*(wine)* espumante *eess-poo-man-tchee*; *(water)* com gás *koŋ gass*
starter	entrada *en-trah-da*
still	*(water)* sem gás *sayŋ gass*
tea	chá *shah*
tip	gorjeta *gor-Jeh-ta*
water	água *ah-gwa*

white coffee	café com leite *ka-feh koη lay-tchee*
white wine	vinho branco *veen-yoo bran-koo*
wine	vinho *veen-yoo*
wine list	carta de vinhos *kar-ta djee veen-yooss*
to drink	beber *beh-beH*
to eat	comer *koh-meH*
to have breakfast	tomar o café da manhã *toh-mar oo ka-feh da man-yaη*
to have dinner	jantar *jan-taH*
to have lunch	almoçar *al-moh-saH*
to order	pedir *peh-djeeH*

Expressing yourself

shall we go and have something to eat?
vamos comer alguma coisa?
vah-mooss koh-mair al-goo-ma koy-za?

do you want to go for a drink?
vamos tomar um drinque?
vah-mooss toh-mar oom dreen-kee?

can you recommend a good restaurant?
você pode me recomendar um bom restaurante?
vo-seh po-djee mee Heh-koh-men-dar oom boη Hess-tow-ran-tchee?

I'm not very hungry
não tenho muita fome
nowη ten-yoo mweeη-ta foh-mee

I'm very hungry
estou com muita fome
eess-toh koη mweeη-ta foh-mee

do you have a table for three people?
tem mesa para três pessoas?
tayη meh-za pah-ra trehss pess-oh-ass?

excuse me! *(to call the waiter)*
por favor!
poor fa-voH!

could you bring me a menu?
posso ver o cardápio?
poss-oo vair oo kar-dah-pee-oo?

cheers!
saúde!
sah-oo-djee!

that was lovely
estava ótimo
eess-tah-va o-tchee-moo

could you bring us an ashtray, please?
(poderia nos trazer) um cinzeiro, por favor?
(poh-deh-ree-a nooss tra-zair) oom seen-zay-roo, poor fa-voH?

where are the toilets, please?
onde fica o toalete?
on-djee fee-ka oo twa-leh-tchee?

Understanding

a quilo	by weight
para levar	takeaway
pagamento antecipado	prepayment

lamento, mas depois das onze (horas) não servimos mais
I'm sorry, we stop serving at 11pm

RESERVING A TABLE

Expressing yourself

I'd like to reserve a table for tomorrow evening
gostaria de reservar uma mesa para amanhã à noite
goss-ta-ree-a djee Heh-zair-var oo-ma meh-za pah-ra ah-man-yaŋ ah noy-tchee

for two people
para duas pessoas
pah-ra doo-ass pess-oh-ass

around 8 o'clock
para as oito (horas)
pah-ra az oy-too (oh-rass)

do you have a table available any earlier than that?
tem alguma mesa disponível mais cedo?
tayŋ al-goo-ma meh-za djeess-poh-nee-vehw ma-eess seh-doo?

I've reserved a table – the name's …
reservei uma mesa, está em nome de …
Heh-zair-vay oo-ma meh-za, eess-ta ayŋ noh-mee djee …

Understanding

reservado	reserved

para que horas?
for what time?

para quantas pessoas?
for how many people?

em nome de quem?
what's the name?

fumante ou não fumante?
smoking or non-smoking?

fez reserva?/tem mesa reservada?
do you have a reservation?

esta mesa, aqui no canto, está bem?
is this table in the corner OK for you?

está lotado, mas se quiser esperar um pouco verei o que posso fazer
I'm afraid we're full at the moment, but if you don't mind waiting a while, I'll see what I can do

ORDERING FOOD

Expressing yourself

yes, we're ready to order
sim, já escolhemos
seeη, Jah eess-kol-yeh-mooss

no, could you give us a few more minutes?
ainda não, você pode nos dar mais alguns minutos?
a-een-da nowη, vo-seh po-djee nooss daH ma-eez al-goonss mee-noo-tooss?

I'd like ...
gostaria de ...
goss-ta-ree-a djee ...

what do you recommend?
o que você recomenda?
oo keh vo-seh Heh-koh-men-da?

I'm not sure, what's "feijoada"?
não tenho certeza, o que é "feijoada"?
nowη ten-yoo sair-teh-za, oo keh eh fay-Joo-ah-da?

I'll have that
pode ser isso então
po-djee sair ee-soo en-towη

what does it come with?
é servido com quê?
eh sair-vee-doo koη keh?

what are today's specials?
quais são os pratos do dia?
kwah-eess sown ooss prah-tooss do djee-a?

what desserts do you have?
que sobremesas vocês têm?
keh soh-breh-meh-zass vo-sess tay-ayn?

some water, please
água, por favor
ah-gwa, poor fa-voH

a bottle of red/white wine
uma garrafa de vinho tinto/branco
oo-ma ga-Hah-fa djee veen-yoo tcheen-too/bran-koo

that's for me
para mim
pah-ra meen

this isn't what I ordered, I wanted …
não foi o que eu pedi, eu queria …
nown foy oo keh eh-oo peh-djee, eh-oo keh-ree-a …

could we have some more bread/another jug of water, please?
(poderia nos trazer) mais pão/mais uma jarra de água, por favor?
(poh-deh-ree-a nooss tra-zair) ma-eess pown/ma-eez oo-ma Jah-Ha djee ah-gwa, poor fa-voH?

Understanding

já escolheu/escolheram?
are you ready to order?

volto mais tarde
I'll come back in a few minutes

lamento, mas acabou …
I'm sorry, we don't have any … left

está tudo bem?
is everything OK?

o que é que você gostaria/vocês gostariam de beber?
what would you like to drink?

você vai/vocês vão querer sobremesa ou café?
would you like dessert or coffee?

BARS AND CAFÉS

Expressing yourself

I'd like ...
gostaria de ...
goss-ta-ree-a djee ...

a Coke®/a diet Coke®
uma Coca-Cola®/uma Coca-Cola® light
oo-ma koh-ka koh-la/oo-ma koh-ka koh-la light

a glass of white/red wine
um copo de vinho branco/tinto
oom koh-poo djee veen-yoo bran-koo/tcheen-too

a black/white coffee
um café preto/com leite
oom ka-feh preh-too/koŋ lay-tchee

a cup of tea
uma xícara de chá
oo-ma shee-ka-ra djee shah

a coffee and a croissant
um café e um croissant
oom ka-feh ee oom kroo-a-san

a cup of hot chocolate
um chocolate quente
oom sho-koh-lah-tchee ken-tchee

the same again, please
o mesmo, por favor
oo meJ-moo, poor fa-voH

Understanding

na mesa	at the table
na parte externa	outside
no balcão	at the bar
sem álcool	non-alcoholic

o que você vai/vocês vão querer/tomar?
what would you like?

esta é uma área para não fumantes
this is a non-smoking area

você se importaria/vocês se importariam de pagar agora?
could I ask you to pay now, please?

EATING AND DRINKING

51

> **Some informal expressions**
>
> **estar de pileque** to be drunk
> **estar de ressaca** to have a hangover

THE BILL

Expressing yourself

the bill, please
a conta, por favor
a kon-ta, poor fa-voH

how much do I owe you?
quanto devo?
kwan-too deh-voo?

do you take credit cards?
aceita cartão de crédito?
a-say-ta kar-towη djee kreh-djee-too?

I think there's a mistake in the bill
acho que há um erro na conta
ah-shoo keh ah oom eh-Hoo na kon-ta

is service included?
o serviço está incluído?
oo sair-vee-soo eess-ta een-kloo-ee-doo?

keep the change
fique com o troco
fee-kee koη oo troh-koo

Understanding

tudo junto ou separado?
are you all paying together?

sim, inclui o serviço
yes, service is included

FOOD AND DRINK

Brazilian cuisine is extremely varied, with a rich mix of African, Italian, Middle-Eastern, Indian and Oriental ingredients. Some dishes can be very spicy, others use exotic vegetables (such as okra, cassava, palm hearts), oils (dende palm oil) and fruits (papaya, mango, passion fruit, guava). Whatever your taste, you are sure to find something you like and a lot more to experiment with!

Churrascarias serve excellent barbecued and roast meats and a **rodízio** restaurant is a good way to grab a fast meal from a fixed-price menu.

If you like fish and seafood, you can find wonderful varieties both in the major cities and along the coast, especially in Bahia.

Prices are generally quite reasonable and portions are generous.

Understanding

à escabeche	with a fried onion sauce
ao ponto	medium
(assado) na brasa	chargrilled, charcoal grilled
assado no forno	roasted; baked
bem-passado	well done
cozido	boiled
defumado	smoked
derretido	melted
dourado	browned
em fatias/em rodelas	sliced
empanado	breaded
fatiado	sliced
fresco	fresh
frio	cold
frito	fried
gratinado	au gratin
grelhado	grilled
levemente refogado	slowly stewed

mal-passado	rare
marinado	marinated
no churrasco	barbecued, grilled
no espeto	on the spit
no ponto	just right
no vapor	steamed
recheado	stuffed
refogado	stewed
sautée	sautéed
seco	dried
temperado	seasoned, dressed

♦ **cafés da manhã e lanches** breakfasts and snacks

açúcar	sugar
bolacha	biscuit
bolo	cake
bolo de arroz	small cake made with rice flour
café	coffee
café com leite	white coffee
café no copo	large white coffee
café preto	black coffee
cafezinho	espresso
calabresa	Calabrian sausage
carioca	small instant coffee
carioca de limão	fresh lemon rind infusion
cereais	cereals
chá	tea
chá de camomila	camomile tea
chá preto	black tea
chá verde	green tea
chocolate quente	hot chocolate
compota	preserve
cortado	espresso with a drop of milk
coxinha de galinha	chicken rissole (shaped like a drumstick)
croissant	croissant
descafeinado	decaffeinated espresso
doce	jam
empada	pasty, small pie
empada de galinha	chicken pasty/pie

expresso	espresso
expresso duplo	double espresso
geléia	jam
iogurte	yoghurt
leite	milk
manteiga	butter
margarina	margarine
marmelada	quince jelly
mortadela	mortadella pork sausage
mel	honey
misto quente	ham and cheese toasted sandwich
nata	thick cream
nega-maluca	chocolate cake
pão	bread
pão-de-leite	brioche
pão-de-queijo	cheese roll
pastel de carne	sausage roll, meat pasty
presunto	dry-cured ham
queijo	cheese
requeijão	cottage cheese
sanduíche	sandwich
salame	salami sausage
suco (de fruta)	(fruit) juice
suco de laranja natural	fresh orange juice
torrada	toast
torrada de queijo e presunto	cheese and ham toasted sandwich
vitamina	smoothie

FOOD AND DRINK

♦ **aperitivos, sopas e entradas** appetizers, soups and starters

A frequent word you will see regarding snack food is **pastel**. Unlike our separate words "pastry", "pie", "fritter", "wrap" etc, this word covers all forms of snacks made from a basic flour dough, whether fried or baked, sweet or savoury.

azeitonas	olives
bolinho de bacalhau	codfish ball
bolinho de siri	deep fried crab cake
broa (de milho)	corn bread
caldo verde	soup made with potatoes, greens and cured sausage
camarão	prawns; shrimps
canja (de galinha)	chicken broth
caruru	shrimps and okra
chouriço	cured pork sausage
coxinha	chicken croquette
creme de cenoura	carrot soup
creme de marisco	seafood soup
croquete	croquettes
embutidos	different types of cured sausages
lingüiça	thin cured pork sausage
melão com presunto	melon with ham
miúdos de frango	chicken giblets served with rice
moela	chicken giblets
mussarela	a type of strong mozzarella made from cow's milk
pamonha	cornmeal wrap with fillings such as cheese (similar to Mexican *tamale*)
pão e manteiga	bread and butter
pasta de queijo	cheese spread
pasta/paté de atum	tuna paté
pasta/paté de sardinha	sardine paté
picles	pickles
presunto	cured ham
queijo	cheese
queijo fresco	fresh cheese (similar to ricotta)
queijo Minas	soft mild fresh cheese
rissole de camarão	shrimp rissoles
rissole de carne/de peixe	meat/hake rissoles
salada de alface	green salad (lettuce only)
salada de palmito	hearts of palm salad
salada mista	mixed salad (usually lettuce, tomatoes and onion)

salada russa	potato salad
salgadinhos	savoury canapés
sopa de abóbora	butternut squash soup
sopa de feijão	bean soup
sopa de grão	chick pea soup
sopa de legumes	vegetable soup
sopa de palmito	hearts of palm soup
sopa de peixe	fish soup

♦ **pratos principais** main courses

One of the staple ingredients of Brazilian cuisine is the black bean (**feijão**) which appears in their most famous dish **feijoada**. Rice is also a must, especially with seafood dishes. In the north, main ingredients are manioc (or cassava) flour and dende palm oil.

peixe, crustáceos e marisco fish, shellfish and seafood

acarajé	bean fritter fried in dende palm oil with shrimp and hot sauce
arroz com camarão	shrimp with rice
arroz com marisco	seafood rice
bacalhau (assado) no forno	baked salt cod, usually with onion, tomatoes and peppers
bacalhau na brasa	chargrilled salt cod
bacalhoada à Portuguesa	boiled dried salt cod, with potatoes, vegetables, boiled eggs and olives
bobó de camarão	manioc, coconut and shrimp with rice
dourado	dorado
espetinho de camarão	shrimp skewers
lagosta	lobster
lula grelhada	grilled squid
lula recheada	stuffed squid
marisco	shellfish
moqueca de camarão	Bahian shrimp stew
moqueca de peixe	fish stew with coconut milk and palm oil

peixe à escabeche	fried fish in a tomato and onion sauce
risoto de camarão	shrimp risotto
seqüência de camarão	shrimps served in a series of different ways (fried, boiled, in garlic, etc.)
siri na casca	crab in its shell
vatapá	shrimp, coconut and garlic porridge dish

carne e aves meat and poultry

à la minuta	steak and egg, accompanied by rice, fries and salad
almôndega	meatballs
arroz à valenciana	rice with chicken and seafood
arroz de cabidela	rice with chicken and chicken blood
arroz de forno	layers of rice, peas and ham with cheese topping
bife	(beef)steak
bife de alcatra	rump steak
cabrito assado	roast kid goat
chuleta	chop
costela de carneiro	lamb chop
cozido à portuguesa	mixed boiled meats, cured sausages and vegetables served with rice
dobradinha	tripe with rice
entrecot	rib-eye steak
escalopes de peru	turkey escalopes
favas à portuguesa	broad bean stew with cured sausage and bacon
feijoada	black bean and pork stew
galinha ao molho pardo	chicken cooked with its own blood
iscas de fígado	fried marinated slivers of liver
jardineira	meat and mixed vegetable stew
leitão assado	roast suckling pig
lombo com farofa	roast pork loin with toasted manioc
lombo de porco	pork loin
pernil/perna de cordeiro	leg of lamb
quibe	lamb kebab
tutu à mineira	black bean puree, with bacon and cassava flour

| **virado à Paulista** | pork chops with rice, fried egg and banana, manioc bean paste and greens |

♦ sobremesas desserts

The majority of sweet desserts are made from eggs, condensed milk and sugar. There are far too many varieties to list here!

ambrosia	egg and milk pudding with cloves and lemon
arroz-doce	rice pudding
bolo inglês	fruit cake
brigadeiro	condensed milk and chocolate
broas de mel	sweet bread made from cornflour, honey and olive oil
cajuzinho	candy-coated peanuts
cassata	cherry and roast almond ice-cream
creme de abacate	avocado cream with lime
creme de leite	egg custard
doce de leite	milk caramel
fios de ovos	egg yolk filaments cooked in syrup
gemada	eggnog
mousse de chocolate	chocolate mousse
pão-de-ló	sponge cake
papos de anjo	small pastries made with syrup, jam, eggs and cinnamon
pavê	cream sponge soaked in liqueur
quindim	sweet made with coconut, egg yolks and sugar
salada de frutas	fruit salad
sorvete	ice cream
suspiro	meringue
torta de bolacha	layers of biscuit and cream egg custard

FOOD AND DRINK

♦ GLOSSARY OF FOOD AND DRINK

abacate avocado
abacaxi pineapple
abóbora pumpkin
açafrão saffron
acompanhamento garnish
adoçante sweetener
agrião watercress
agridoce sweet and sour
água mineral mineral water
água tônica tonic water
aipo celery
alcachofra artichoke
alcaparras capers
alecrim rosemary
alface lettuce
alho garlic
alho-poró leek
ameixa plum
amêndoa almond
amêndoas salgadas salted almonds
amendoim peanut
amido potato starch
amora blackberry
anchova anchovy
aperitivo aperitif
arraia skate
arroz rice
arroz branco plain rice
aspargo asparagus
assado roast
atum tuna
avelã hazelnut
azeite olive oil
azeite de dendê dende oil
bacalhau (salgado) dried salt cod
bagaço strong clear spirit from cane sugar
banana frita fried banana
banha lard
batatas potatoes
batatas fritas chips; crisps
batida smoothie
bebida drink
beringela aubergine
besugo sea bream
beterraba beetroot

bife de atum tuna steak
biscoito biscuit, cookie
bolinho de carne bread stuffed with meat
brócolis broccoli
caça game
cação dogfish
cacau cocoa
cachaça white sugar-cane rum
cachorro-quente hot-dog
cajus cashew nuts
calda syrup
caldo stock
camarão seco dried shrimp
camarão-de-água-doce crayfish
canela cinnamon
caranguejo crab
carne bovina beef
carne de porco pork
carne de vaca beef
carne picada minced meat
carneiro lamb
carnes frias cold meats
caseiro homemade
castanhas chestnuts
catupiry soft processed cheese for pizzas
cavala mackerel
cebola onion
cebolinha chive
cenoura carrot
cereja cherry
cerveja beer
cerveja preta stout
chocolate chocolate
chope draft beer
cidra cider
clara de ovo egg white
coco coconut
codorna quail
coentro coriander
cogumelo mushroom
comida food
cominho cumin
congro conger eel
conhaque brandy
conservante preservative

copo glass
coração heart
corvina black bream
costeleta chop
couve curly kale, collard greens
couve de Bruxelas Brussels sprouts
couve-flor cauliflower
coxa de frango drumstick
cravinho clove
cru raw
crustáceos shellfish
damasco apricot
enguia eel
erva-doce aniseed
ervilhas peas
espaguete spaghetti
especiaria spice
espesso thick
espeto skewer, kebab
espinafre spinach
espinha fishbone
espumante light, slightly sparkling wine
estragão tarragon
farinha flour
farinheira sausage made with flour, pork fat, paprika and herbs
farofa manioc meal
favas broad beans
feijão branco white bean; butter bean
feijão preto black bean
feijão verde green bean
fígado liver
figo fig
flocos de aveia porridge oats
flocos de milho cornflakes
framboesa raspberry
frango chicken
fruta fruit
fruta da época fruit in season
funcho fennel
galeto barbecued chicken
galinha chicken
ganso goose
gelo ice
gema de ovo egg yolk
gengibre ginger
goiaba guava

grão chick peas
groselha redcurrant
guaraná a tropical berry for soft drinks and flavouring
guarnição garnish
hortelã mint
imperial schooner of beer
javali wild boar
lagosta lobster
laranja orange
lebre hare
legumes vegetables
leite milk
leite creme custard
leite desnatado skimmed milk
leite integral whole milk
leite semidesnatado semi-skimmed milk
lentilhas lentils
lima lime
limão type of lemon (green and similar to a lime)
louro bay leaf
lúcio pike
maçã apple
maionese mayonnaise
mamão papaya
mandioca frita fried yuca
manjericão basil
maracujá passion fruit
marisco seafood
marmelo quince
massa pasta; dough
massa folhada puff pastry
medalhão medallion
melancia watermelon
menta mint
mexilhões mussels
migalhas crumbs
milho corn
milho (doce) sweetcorn
molho sauce
morango strawberry
morcela black pudding
mostarda mustard
nabo turnip
natas cream
nectarina nectarine

noz moscada nutmeg
nozes walnuts
óleo cooking oil
omelete omelette
orégano oregano
osso bone
ostra oyster
ovas fish roe
ovo egg
ovo cozido/duro hard boiled egg
ovo frito fried egg
ovo quente soft-boiled egg
ovos mexidos scrambled eggs
pão bread; roll
pão de centeio rye bread
pão de fôrma sandwich loaf
pão integral wholemeal bread
papo-seco roll
páprica paprika
pargo sea bream
passa raisin
pastel small cake
pato duck
peixe-espada scabbard fish
pepino cucumber
pêra pear
perdiz partridge
pêssego peach
picante hot, spicy
pimenta pepper
pimenta em grão peppercorns
pimenta-malagueta chilli pepper
pimentão-doce paprika
pimentão verde green pepper
pinhão pine nuts

pipoca popcorn
pudim pudding
puré mashed potatoes
rabanada French toast
rabanete radish
refrigerante soft drink
rim kidney
rodovalho turbot
sal salt
salchicha sausage
salgadinho savoury snack
salgado salted
salmão salmon
salmão defumado smoked salmon
salpicão type of cured pork sausage
salsa parsley
salsichão lean cured pork sausage
sementes seeds
sépia cuttlefish
tainha red mullet
tamboril monkfish
tangerina tangerine
tempero seasoning, dressing
tomate tomato
tomilho thyme
toucinho streaky bacon
tremoços lupini beans
truta trout
uvas grapes
vinagre vinegar
vinho wine
vinho da casa house wine
vinho de mesa table wine
vinho do Porto port
vinho moscatel Muscatel wine

GOING OUT

There is no shortage of nightlife in most Brazilian towns and cities and the warm climate means that you can stay out late – most Brazilians don't even leave the house until after 10pm.

There is a strong tradition of bars and nightclubs with live music. In São Paulo the main centres are Bixiga, Jardins, Itaim Bibi, Vila Olímpia, Vila Madalena and Pinheiros – the best way to find out what is on is to consult the weekly Veja, or the Guia Internet websites (São Paulo – www.guiasp.com.br – and Rio – www.guiarj.com.br). You won't have problems finding a disco, but if you feel adventurous and want to dance with the locals you could go to a **gafieira**, a dance hall where all classes meet.

Cinemas are quite cheap. Films are normally the latest releases and are subtitled for Portuguese so there is no problem seeing an English-language film. Head for any large shopping centre and you will find a cinema complex there. A good place to watch arthouse films in São Paulo, as well as Brazilian folk and New Wave music, is the Centro Cultural de São Paulo near the Vergueiro metro station. Rio de Janeiro holds the international film festival, Rio-Cine, for ten days each November at the Convention Centre of the Hotel Nacional in São Conrado. Rio is also famous for jazz music and holds the Free Jazz Festival there in late August or early September.

Both Rio and São Paulo have a strong theatre, opera and classical music tradition with world-class facilities – even in the heart of the Amazon, at Manaus, there is a famous opera house.

Eating and drinking are social events and, given the climate, you usually go out on the town to enjoy a party. However, if invited to a party in somebody's flat, remember to take a bottle with you.

The basics

ballet	balé *ba-leh*
band	banda *ban-da*
bar	bar *baH*

cinema	cinema *see-neh-ma*
circus	circo *seer-koo*
classical music	música clássica *moo-zee-ka klass-ee-ka*
club	discoteca *djeess-koh-teh-ka*
concert	concerto *kon-sair-too*
funfair	feira popular *fay-ra poh-poo-laH*
festival	festival *fess-tchee-vahw*
film	filme *feel-mee*
folk music	música popular *moo-zee-ka poh-poo-laH*
group	grupo *groo-poo*
jazz	jazz *Jass*
modern dance	dança moderna *dan-sa moh-dair-na*
musical	musical *moo-zee-kahw*
opera	ópera *o-peh-ra*
party	festa *fess-ta*
play	peça (de teatro) *pess-a (djee tchee-ah-troo)*
pop music	música pop *moo-zee-ka pop*
rock music	(música) rock *(moo-zee-ka) Hoh-kee*
show	espetáculo *eess-peh-tah-koo-loo*
subtitled film	filme legendado/com legendas *feel-mee leh-Jen-dah-doo/kon leh-Jen-dass*
theatre	teatro *tchee-ah-troo*
ticket	entrada *en-trah-da*
to book	reservar *Heh-zair-vaH*
to go out	sair *sa-eeH*

SUGGESTIONS AND INVITATIONS

Expressing yourself

where can we go?
onde podemos ir?
on-djee poh-deh-mooss eeH?

what do you want to do?
o que você quer *(sg)*/vocês querem *(pl)* fazer?
oo keh vo-seh kair/vo-sess keh-rayŋ fa-zeH?

shall we go for a drink?
vamos tomar um drinque?
*vah-mooss toh-**mar** oom **dreen**-kee?*

what are you doing tonight?
o que você vai *(sg)*/vocês vão *(pl)* fazer hoje à noite?
*oo keh vo-**seh** va-ee/vo-**sess** vowŋ fa-**zair** oh-Jee ah **noy**-tchee?*

do you have plans?
você já tem *(sg)*/vocês já têm *(pl)* planos?
*vo-**seh** Jah tayŋ/vo-**sess** Jah **tay**-ayŋ **plah**-nooss?*

would you like to ...?
gostaria *(sg)*/gostariam *(pl)* de ...?
*goss-ta-**ree**-a/goss-ta-**ree**-owŋ djee...?*

we were thinking of going to ...
estávamos pensando em ir a ...
*eess-**tah**-va-mooss pen-**san**-doo ayŋ eer a ...*

I can't today, but maybe some other time
hoje eu não posso, mas talvez outro dia
*oh-Jee **eh**-oo nowŋ **poss**-oo, mass tal-**vess** oh-troo **djee**-a*

I'm not sure I can make it
não sei se vou poder ir
*nowŋ say see voh poh-**dair** eeH*

I'd love to ...
adoraria ...
*a-doh-ra-**ree**-a ...*

ARRANGING TO MEET

Expressing yourself

where/what time shall we meet?
onde/a que horas nos encontramos?
***on**-djee/a keh **oh**-rass nooss en-kon-**trah**-mooss?*

would it be possible to meet a bit later?
poderia ser um pouco mais tarde?
*poh-deh-**ree**-a sair oom **poh**-koo ma-eess **tar**-djee?*

I have to meet ... at nine
tenho um encontro marcado com ... às nove
***ten**-yoo oom en-**kon**-troo mar-**kah**-doo koŋ ... ass **noh**-vee*

I don't know where it is but I'll find it on the map
não sei onde é, mas vejo no mapa
nowŋ say on-djee eh, mass veh-Joo noo mah-pa

see you tomorrow night
até amanhã (à noite)
a-teh a-man-yaŋ (ah noy-tchee)

I'll meet you later, I have to stop by the hotel first
até mais tarde, tenho primeiro que passar pelo hotel
a-teh ma-eess tar-djee, ten-yoo pree-may-roo keh pass-aH peh-loo oh-tehw

I'll call you if there's a change of plan
eu telefono se tiver alguma mudança de planos
eh-oo teh-leh-foh-noo see tchee-vair al-goo-ma moo-dahn-sa djee plah-nooss

are you going to eat beforehand?
comemos alguma coisa antes?
koh-meh-mooss al-goo-ma koy-za an-tcheess?

sorry I'm late
desculpe, estou atrasado
djeess-kool-pee, eess-toh a-tra-zah-doo

Understanding

tudo bem com você?
is that OK with you?

venho buscar você às oito
I'll come and pick you up about 8

encontro você lá
I'll meet you there

podemos nos encontrar lá fora
we can meet outside

vou lhe dar o meu número e você pode me ligar amanhã
I'll give you my number and you can call me tomorrow

FILMS, SHOWS AND CONCERTS

Expressing yourself

is there a guide to what's on?
há algum guia de espetáculos?
ah al-goom ghee-a djee eess-peh-tah-koo-looss?

I'd like three tickets for ...
queria três entradas para ...
*keh-**ree**-a trehss en-**trah**-dass **pah**-ra ...*

two tickets, please
duas entradas, por favor
*doo-ass en-**trah**-dass, poor fa-**voH***

I've seen the trailer
vi o trailer
*vee oo **tray**-lair*

it's called ...
chama-se ...
shah-ma-see ...

what time does it start?
a que horas começa?
*a keh **oh**-rass koh-**meh**-sa?*

I'd like to go and see a show
gostaria de ir ver um espetáculo
*goss-ta-**ree**-a djee eeH vair oom eess-peh-**tah**-koo-loo*

I'll find out whether there are still tickets available
vou ver se ainda há entradas
*voh veh see a-**een**-da ah en-**trah**-dass*

do we need to book in advance?
precisa de reserva antecipada?
*preh-**see**-za djee Heh-**zair**-va an-tchee-see-**pah**-da?*

how long is it on for?
até quando vai estar em cartaz?
*a-teh kwan-doo **vah**-ee eess-**tar** ayŋ kar-**tass**?*

are there tickets for another day?
há entradas para outro dia?
*ah en-**trah**-dass **pah**-ra **oh**-troo **djee**-a?*

I'd like to go to a bar with some live music
gostaria de ir a um bar com música ao vivo
*goss-ta-**ree**-a djee eer a oom baH koŋ **moo**-zee-ka ow **vee**-voo*

are there any free concerts?
há algum concerto que seja de graça?
*ah al-**goom** kon-**sair**-too keh **seh**-Ja djee **grah**-sa?*

what sort of music is it?
que tipo de música que é?
*keh **tchee**-poo djee **moo**-zee-ka keh eh?*

Understanding

auditório	concert hall
bilheteria	box office
cinemateca	filmhouse
em cartaz a partir de ...	on general release from ...
estréia	first showing
lotação esgotada	sold out
reservas	bookings
sala de espetáculos	concert hall/theatre
sessão	showing
teatro de revista	revue

é um concerto ao ar livre
it's an open-air concert

teve críticas muito boas
it's had very good reviews

estréia na próxima semana
it comes out next week

começa às oito no Palace
it's on at 8pm at the Palace

essa sessão está esgotada
that showing's sold out

está esgotado até ...
it's all booked up until ...

não é preciso reservar
there's no need to book in advance

favor desligar os celulares
please turn off your mobile phones

PARTIES AND CLUBS

Expressing yourself

I'm having a little leaving party tonight
vou dar uma festa de despedida hoje à noite
voh dar oo-ma fess-ta djee djeess-peh-djee-da oh-Jee ah noy-tchee

should I bring something to drink?
levo alguma coisa para beber?
leh-voo al-goo-ma koy-za pah-ra beh-beH?

we could go to a club afterwards
depois podíamos ir dançar um pouco
djee-poyss poh-djee-a-mooss eeH dan-sar oom poh-koo

do you have to pay to get in?
precisa pagar para entrar?
preh-see-za pa-gaH pah-ra en-traH?

I have to meet someone inside
marquei encontro com alguém lá dentro
mar-kay en-kon-troo koŋ al-gayŋ lah den-troo

will you let me back in when I come back?
posso entrar de novo quando eu voltar?
poss-oo en-traH djee noh-voo kwan-doo eh-oo vol-taH?

do you come here often?
você vem aqui muitas vezes?
vo-seh vayŋ a-kee mweeŋ-tass veh-zeess?

can I buy you a drink?
posso lhe pagar um drinque?
poss-oo lyee pa-gar oom dreen-kee?

thanks, but I'm with my boyfriend
não, obrigada, estou com meu namorado
nowŋ oh-bree-gah-da, eess-toh koŋ meh-oo na-moh-rah-doo

no thanks, I don't smoke
não, obrigado *(m)*/obrigada *(f)*, não fumo
nowŋ oh-bree-gah-doo/oh-bree-gah-da, nowŋ foo-moo

GOING OUT

Understanding

bebida grátis	free drink
vestiário	cloakroom
15 reais depois da meia-noite	15 reals after midnight

tem uma festa na casa do Pedro
there's a party at Pedro's place

quer dançar?	**posso lhe comprar uma bebida?**
do you want to dance?	can I buy you a drink?
tem fogo?	**tem um cigarro?**
have you got a light?	have you got a cigarette?
a gente pode se ver de novo?	**posso levar você para casa?**
can we see each other again?	can I see you home?

69

TOURISM AND SIGHTSEEING

The possibilities for the tourist in Brazil are endless: from big-city sightseeing in Rio and São Paulo, to the more adventurous ecotourism of the Amazon rainforests, the vast UNESCO wetland reserve of the Pantanal, the Abrolhos Sea National Park with its humpback whales or the Iguaçu Falls, the widest group of waterfalls in the world; from the historical sights of old Rio and the Gothic buildings of the gold-mining town of Ouro Preto, to the colonial architecture of the north-east and Salvador.

Rio is probably the most popular tourist destination. The Rio de Janeiro Convention and Visitors Bureau (**www.rioconventionbureau.com.br**) has all the information you will need. Must-sees are, of course, the Statue of Christ the Redeemer on top of the Corcovado hunchback mountain giving fantastic views over the city and that other landmark, Sugarloaf Mountain, which can be reached by cable car. For more relaxing sightseeing visit the Arco do Teles, with its restaurants, cafés and bossa nova and samba bars. More cultural sights include the National History Museum with its exhibits from colonial times and the Museu Nacional de Belas Artes with its display of leading 19th- and 20th-century artists. Carnival has to be the best time to visit when the city comes to a halt and parties non-stop for four days with its impressive samba displays and processions!

São Paulo also has its great art museums, including the Contemporary Art Museum and the Museu de Arte de São Paulo, with one of the finest art collections of European and Brazilian art. Another pleasant place to spend the day is the Ibirapuera Park with its lakes, Japanese pavilion, Planetarium, and many museums of folklore and modern art. Old São Paulo in the historical centre boasts the beautiful Municipal Theatre, home to opera, music and ballet, Anhangabau Valley and the Pátio do Colégio where the city was founded.

The basics

ancient	antigo/antiga *an-tchee-goo/an-tchee-ga*
antique	antigüidade *an-tchee-gwee-dah-djee*
area	região *HeJ-yowη*
cable car	teleférico *teh-leh-feh-ree-koo*
castle	castelo *kass-teh-loo*
cathedral	catedral *ka-teh-drahw*
century	século *seh-koo-loo*
church	igreja *ee-greh-Ja*
ecotourism	ecoturismo *eh-koh-too-reeJ-moo*
exhibition	exposição *eess-poh-zee-sowη*
gallery	galeria de arte *ga-leh-ree-a djee ar-tchee*
lake	lago *lah-goo*
modern art	arte moderna *ar-tchee moh-dair-na*
mosque	mesquita *mess-kee-ta*
museum	museu *moo-zeh-oo*
painting	quadro *kwah-droo*, pintura *peen-too-ra*
park	parque *par-kee*
quarter	bairro *by-Hoo*
rainforest	floresta pluvial *floh-ress-ta ploo-vee-ow*
ruins	ruínas *Hoo-ee-nass*
sculpture	escultura *eess-kool-too-ra*
statue	estátua *eess-tat-wa*
street map	mapa de ruas *mah-pa djee Hoo-ass*
synagogue	sinagoga *see-na-goh-ga*
tour guide	guia (turístico) *ghee-a (too-reess-tchee-koo)*
tourist	turista *too-reess-ta*
tourist information centre	posto de informações turísticas *poss-too djee een-for-ma-soyηss too-reess-tchee-kass*
town centre	centro da cidade *sen-troo da see-dah-djee*
waterfall	queda d'água *keh-da dah-gwa*

Expressing yourself

I'd like some information on …
eu gostaria de algumas informações sobre …
eh-oo goss-ta-ree-a djee al-goo-mass een-for-ma-soyηss soh-bree …

can you tell me where the tourist information centre is?
você pode me dizer onde fica o posto de turismo?
vo-seh po-djee mee djee-zair on-djee fee-ka oo poss-too djee too-reeJ-moo?

do you have a street map of the town?
tem um mapa da cidade?
tayŋ oom mah-pa da see-dah-djee?

what is there worth visiting?
o que há de interessante para visitar?
oo keh ah djee een-teh-reh-san-tchee pah-ra vee-zee-taH?

can you show me where it is on the map?
você pode me indicar onde fica no mapa?
vo-seh po-djee mee een-djee-kar on-djee fee-ka noo mah-pa?

how do you get there?   is it free?
como é que chego lá?   a entrada é grátis?
koh-moo eh keh sheh-goo lah? a en-trah-da eh grah-tcheess?

when was it built?
quando foi construído *(m)*/construída *(f)*?
kwan-doo foy kon-stroo-ee-doo/kon-stroo-ee-da?

Understanding

aberto	open
barroco/barroca	Baroque
centro da cidade	city centre
circuito turístico	tourist trail
colonial	colonial
entrada livre	admission free
favela	shanty town
fechado para obras	closed for renovation
miradouro	viewpoint
obras de restauração	restoration work
patrimônio da humanidade	world heritage site
visita guiada	guided tour
vista panorâmica	panoramic view
você está aqui	you are here *(on a map)*
zona histórica	old town
zona para pedestres	pedestrian precinct

você vai ter que perguntar quando chegar lá
you'll have to ask when you get there

a próxima visita guiada começa às duas (horas)
the next guided tour starts at 2 o'clock

MUSEUMS, EXHIBITIONS AND MONUMENTS

Expressing yourself

I've heard there's a very good ... exhibition on at the moment
ouvi dizer que neste momento há uma exposição muito boa sobre ...
oh-vee djee-zeH keh ness-tchee moh-men-too ah oo-ma eess-poh-zee-sown mween-too boh-a soh-bree ...

how much is it to get in?
quanto custa a entrada?
kwan-too kooss-ta a en-trah-da?

is this ticket valid for the exhibition as well?
esta entrada também vale para a exposição?
ess-ta en-trah-da tam-bayn vah-lee pah-ra a eess-poh-zee-sown?

are there any discounts for students?
há desconto para estudantes?
ah djeess-kon-too pah-ra eess-too-dan-tcheess?

is it open on Sundays?
abre aos domingos?
ah-bree owss doh-meen-gooss?

two concessions and one full price, please
duas entradas com desconto e uma normal, por favor
doo-ass en-trah-dass kon djeess-kon-too ee oo-ma nor-mahw, poor fa-voH

I have a student card
tenho carteira de estudante
ten-yoo kar-tay-ra djee eess-too-dan-tchee

Understanding

exposição permanente   permanent exhibition

TOURISM, SIGHTSEEING

exposição temporária	temporary exhibition
guia de áudio	audioguide
guichê	ticket office
não tocar	please do not touch
proibido tirar fotografias	no photography
proibido usar flash	no flash photography
sentido da visita	this way
silêncio, por favor	silence, please

a entrada (para o museu) custa …
admission to the museum costs …

esta entrada também vale para a exposição
this ticket also allows you access to the exhibition

você tem carteira de estudante?
do you have a student card?

GIVING YOUR IMPRESSIONS

Expressing yourself

it's beautiful
é lindo *(m)*/linda *(f)*
eh leen-doo/leen-da

it's fantastic
é fantástico *(m)*/fantástica *(f)*
eh fan-tass-tchee-koo/fan-tass-tchee-ka

I really enjoyed it
gostei muito
goss-tay mweeŋ-too

I didn't like it that much
não gostei muito
nowŋ goss-tay mweeŋ-too

it was a bit boring
foi um pouco chato *(m)*/chata *(f)*
foy oom poh-koo shah-too/shah-ta

it's expensive for what it is
é muito caro para o que é
eh mweeŋ-too kah-roo pah-ra oo keh eh

I'm not really a fan of modern art
não gosto muito de arte moderna
nowŋ goss-too mweeŋ-too djee ar-tchee moh-dair-na

it's very touristy
é muito turístico *(m)*/turística *(f)*
eh mweeŋ-too too-reess-tchee-koo/too-reess-tchee-ka

it was really crowded
havia muita gente
a-vee-a mweeŋ-ta Jen-tchee

we didn't go in the end, the queue was too long
acabamos não indo, a fila era muito longa
a-ka-bah-mooss nowŋ een-doo, a fee-la eh-ra mweeŋ-too lon-ga

we didn't have time to see everything
não tivemos tempo de ver tudo
nowŋ tchee-veh-mooss tem-poo djee veH too-doo

Understanding

famoso/famosa	famous
pitoresco/pitoresca	picturesque
típico/típica	typical
tradicional	traditional

você tem/vocês têm que ver …
you really must go and see …

eu recomendo que você vá/vocês vão a ...
I recommend going to …

a vista da cidade é lindíssima
the view of the city is beautiful

ficou muito turístico/turística
it's become a bit too touristy

a costa está completamente arruinada
the coast has been completely ruined

SPORTS AND GAMES

Football (**futebol**) is by far the most popular sport in Brazil, with many World Cup wins to its name and famous players such as Pelé and Ronaldo. The Maracanã stadium in Rio is one of the largest in the world; nearly everybody plays football and watches it on TV and its revenues help support all the other major sports.

Brazil has also had its other champions in sports such as grand prix racing, tennis, basketball, sailing and equestrianism.

A unique sport (a cross between martial arts and dancing) is **Capoeira** which now has aficionados throughout the world.

One other major sporting obsession in Brazil is volleyball and all its variations. This is not surprising with so many good beaches to play on all year round, and the Brazilians have had time to invent their own versions, such as **footvolley** (feet and hands), **biribol** (in the water) and the brand new **bossaball**, which is footvolley combined with Capoeira played on trampolines and inflatables, and all to the rhythm of samba music!

The basics

ball	bola *bo-la*
basketball	basquete *bass-keh-tchee*
board game	jogo de tabuleiro *Joh-goo djee ta-boo-lay-roo*
cards	cartas *kar-tass*
chess	xadrez *sha-dress*
cycling	ciclismo *see-kleeJ-moo*
diving	mergulho *mair-gool-yoo*
football	futebol *foo-tchee-bow*
goal	gol *gow*
goalkeeper	goleiro *goh-lay-roo*
hang gliding	asa-delta *ah-za del-ta*
match	jogo *Joh-goo*
pool	(game) bilhar *beel-yaH*
paragliding	vôo de parapente *voh-oo djee pa-ra-pen-tchee*

referee	árbitro *ar-bee-troo*, juiz *Joo-eess*
riding	equitação *eh-kee-ta-sown*
sailing	(navegação a) vela *(na-veh-ga-sown ah) veh-la*
sport	esporte *eess-por-tchee*
surfing	surfe *soor-fee*
swimming	nadar *na-daH*, natação *na-ta-sown*
swimming pool	piscina *pee-see-na*
table football	pebolim *peh-boh-leen*
team	time *tchee-mee*
tennis	tênis *teh-neess*
volleyball	vôlei *voh-lay*
water skiing	esqui aquático *eess-kee a-kwa-tchee-koo*
to go sailing	velejar *veh-leh-JaH*
to have a game of ...	disputar uma partida de ... *djeess-poo-tar oo-ma par-tchee-da djee ...*
to play	jogar *Joh-gaH*

Expressing yourself

I'd like to hire ... for an hour
gostaria de alugar ... por uma hora
goss-ta-ree-a djee a-loo-gaH ... poor oo-ma oh-ra

are there ... lessons available?
é possível ter aulas de ...?
eh poh-see-vehw tair ow-lass djee ...?

how much is it per person per hour?
quanto custa por hora por pessoa?
kwan-too kooss-ta poor oh-ra poor pess-oh-a?

I'm not very sporty
não pratico muito esporte
nown pra-tchee-koo mween-too eess-por-tchee

I've never done it before
nunca tentei
noon-ka ten-tay

I've done it once or twice, a long time ago
tentei uma ou duas vezes, faz muito tempo
ten-tay oo-ma oh doo-ass veh-zeess, fass mween-too tem-poo

I'm exhausted!
estou exausto *(m)*/exausta *(f)*!
eess-**toh** eh-**zowss**-too/eh-**zowss**-ta!

I'd like to go and watch a football match
gostaria de assistir a um jogo de futebol
goss-ta-**ree**-a djee ass-eess-**teer** ah oom **Joh**-goo djee foo-tchee-**bow**

we played …
jogamos …
Joh-**gah**-mooss …

Understanding

… aluga-se … for hire

já tem alguma experiência, ou é a primeira vez?
do you have any experience, or are you a complete beginner?

precisa fazer um depósito de …
there is a deposit of …

o seguro é obrigatório e custa …
insurance is compulsory and costs …

FOOTBALL

Expressing yourself

where can I get a ticket for the game?
onde eu posso comprar ingresso para o jogo?
on-djee **eh**-oo **poss**-oo kom-**prar** een-**gress**-oo **pah**-ra oo **joh**-goo

I'd like a ticket for the upper/lower terraces
quero um ingresso para a arquibancada superior/inferior
kair-oo oom een-**gress**-oo **pah**-ra a ar-kee-ban-**kah**-da soo-peh-ree-o**H**/eem-feh-ree-o**H**

does this stadium have a covered area?
este estádio tem área coberta?
ehss-tchee eess-**tad**-yoo tayŋ **ah**-ree-a koo-**bair**-ta?

is there parking at the stadium?
o estádio tem estacionamento?
oo eess-tad-yoo tayη eess-tass-yoh-na-men-too?

where are the ticket booths at the stadium?
onde ficam as bilheterias do estádio?
on-djee fee-kown ass beel-yeh-teh-ree-ass doo eess-tad-yoo?

how much are the comfortable seats?
quanto custam as cadeiras?
kwan-too kooss-town ass ka-day-rass?

where is entrance gate 8?
onde fica o portão 8?
on-djee fee-ka oo por-town oy-too?

how early do we need to arrive before the match starts?
tem que chegar quanto tempo antes da partida?
tayη keh sheh-gaH kwan-too tem-poo an-tcheess da par-tchee-da?

does anyone have a football?
alguém tem uma bola?
al-gayη tayη oo-ma bo-la?

which team do you support?
para que time você torce?
pah-ra keh tchee-mee vo-seh tor-see?

I support ...
torço para ...
tor-soo pah-ra ...

Understanding

cadeiras numeradas	numbered seating
intervalo	half-time
primeiro/segundo tempo	first/second half

faltam dez minutos para acabar o primeiro tempo
there's only ten minutes to the end of the first half

é melhor levar uma almofadinha para o estádio
it's a good idea to take a cushion with you to the stadium

OTHER SPORTS

Expressing yourself

where can we hire bikes?
onde podemos alugar bicicletas?
on-djee poh-deh-mooss a-loo-gaH bee-see-kleh-tass?

are there any cycle paths in this area?
tem alguma ciclovia na região?
tayŋ al-goo-ma see-kloh-vee-a na HeJ-yowŋ?

is there an open-air swimming pool?
tem alguma piscina ao ar livre?
tayŋ al-goo-ma pee-see-na ow aH lee-vree?

I've never been diving before
nunca pratiquei mergulho
noon-ka pra-tchee-kay mair-gool-yoo

I'd like to take beginners' sailing lessons
gostaria de ter algumas aulas de vela para principiantes
goss-ta-ree-a djee tair al-goo-mass ow-lass djee veh-la pah-ra preen-seep-yan-tcheess

can you recommend any good walks in the area?
pode me recomendar algum passeio a pé na zona?
po-djee mee heh-koh-men-dar al-goom pass-ay-oo a peh na zoh-na?

we're looking for a short walk somewhere round here
gostariamos de dar um pequeno passeio a pé por aqui perto
goss-ta-ree-a-mooss djee dar oom peh-keh-noo pass-ay-oo a peh poor a-kee pair-too

is it very steep?
tem que subir muito?
tayŋ keh soo-beeH mweeŋ-too?

Understanding

há uma quadra de tênis perto da estação
there's a public tennis court not far from the station

a quadra de tênis está ocupada
the tennis court's being used

é a primeira vez que você monta (a cavalo)?
is this the first time you've been horse-riding?

você sabe nadar?
can you swim?

você joga basquete?
do you play basketball?

INDOOR GAMES

SPORTS AND GAMES

Expressing yourself

shall we have a game of cards?
vamos jogar cartas?
vah-mooss Joh-gar kar-tass?

does anyone know any good card games?
alguém conhece um bom jogo de cartas?
al-gayŋ kon-yeh-see oom boŋ Joh-goo djee kar-tass?

it's your turn
é a sua vez
eh a soo-a vess

Understanding

sabe jogar xadrez?
do you know how to play chess?

tem um baralho?
do you have a pack of cards?

> **Some informal expressions**
> **estou podre de cansado/cansada** I'm totally knackered
> **ele acabou comigo** he absolutely thrashed me

SHOPPING

The opening hours for most shops and businesses are from 9am to 6pm, with a long lunch break from noon to 2pm. Saturday closing is at noon, with only a few shops open late on a Sunday. Shopping malls, nevertheless, are open from 10am to 10pm, from Monday to Saturday – they are open on Sundays mainly for food and the cinema, while other shops can vary. Malls are also air-conditioned, which makes them very pleasant places to be in the hot weather!

Clothing and shoes are especially good quality and reasonably priced, so why not take advantage and start blending in with the crowd, both in town as well as on the beach! Get yourself a pair of **Havaianas®** (flip-flops) – the Brazilians wear them all the time. Food is also excellent value, with an enormous variety of fruit and vegetables. Popular supermarkets in Brazil include Carrefour, Bompreço, Pão de Açúcar and Comprebem. Better still, if you are away from the big city centres, go and explore one of the weekly street markets (**feiras** – usually in the downtown or port area) where you can find even greater variety and fresher produce, as well as meeting some of the friendly locals.

On the beach you don't have to move, as the vendors come to you selling snacks and drinks. And talking of relaxing shopping, a good souvenir to buy is a hammock (**rede**), unusual but practical!

Some informal expressions

custa os olhos da cara it costs an arm and a leg
é um roubo! that's a rip-off!
é uma pechincha! it's a bargain!
não tenho um tostão I'm broke
ver vitrines to go window shopping

The basics

bakery   padaria *pa-da-ree-a*

butcher's	açougue *a-soh-ghee*
cash desk	caixa *ka-ee-sha*
cheap	barato/barata *ba-rah-too/ba-rah-ta*
checkout	caixa *ka-ee-sha*
clothes	roupa *Hoh-pa*
department store	loja de departamentos *loh-Ja djee deh-par-ta-men-tooss*
expensive	caro/cara *kah-roo/kah-ra*
gram	grama *grah-ma*
greengrocer's	verdureiro *vair-doo-ray-roo*, quitanda *kee-tan-da*
handicraft	artesanato *ar-teh-za-nah-too*
hypermarket	hipermercado *ee-pair-mair-kah-doo*
kilo	quilo *kee-loo*
present	presente *preh-zen-tchee*
price	preço *preh-soo*
receipt	recibo *heh-see-boo*
refund	reembolso *Heh-em-bol-soo*
sales	liquidação *lee-kee-da-sowη*
sales assistant	vendedor/vendedora *ven-deh-doH/ven-deh-doh-ra*
shop	loja *loh-Ja*
shopping centre	shopping center *sho-peeη sen-tair*
souvenir	lembrança *lem-bran-sa*
street market	feira *fay-ra*
supermarket	supermercado *soo-pair-mair-kah-doo*
to buy	comprar *kom-praH*
to cost	custar *kooss-taH*
to go shopping	ir fazer compras *eeH fa-zeH kom-prass*
to pay	pagar *pa-gaH*
to refund	reembolsar *Heh-em-bol-saH*
to sell	vender *ven-deH*

SHOPPING

Expressing yourself

is there a supermarket near here?
há algum supermercado aqui perto?
ah al-goom soo-pair-mair-kah-doo a-kee pair-too?

where can I buy ...?
onde posso comprar ...?
on-djee poss-oo kom-praH ...?

do you sell ...?
você tem ...?
vo-seh tayη ...?

I'd like ...
eu gostaria de ...
eh-oo goss-ta-ree-a djee ...

I'm looking for ...
estou procurando ...
eess-toh proh-koo-ran-doo ...

do you know where I might find some ...?
você sabe onde eu posso encontrar ...?
vo-seh sah-bee on-djee eh-oo poss-oo en-kon-traH ...?

how much is this?
quanto custa (isto)?
kwan-too kooss-ta (eess-too)?

I'll take it
vou querer
voh keh-reH

I haven't got much money
não tenho muito dinheiro
nowη ten-yoo mweeη-too djeen-yay-roo

I haven't got enough money
não tenho dinheiro que chegue
nowη ten-yoo djeen-yay-roo keh sheh-ghee

that's everything, thanks
é isso, obrigado *(m)*/obrigada *(f)*
eh ee-soo, oh-bree-gah-doo/oh-bree-gah-da

can I have a (plastic) bag?
poderia me dar um saco (de plástico)?
poh-deh-ree-a mee dar oom sah-koo (djee plass-tchee-koo)?

I think you've made a mistake with my change
acho que você se enganou no troco
ah-shoo keh vo-seh see en-ga-noh noo troh-koo

Understanding

aberto das ... às ...	open from ... to ...
fechado aos domingos/entre às 13h e às 15h	closed Sundays/1pm to 3pm
horário de funcionamento	opening hours
liquidação	sales
promoção	special offer

84

mais alguma coisa?
will there be anything else?

quer um saco?
would you like a bag?

PAYING

Expressing yourself

where do I pay?
onde eu pago?
on-djee eh-oo pah-goo?

how much do I owe you?
quanto devo?
kwan-too deh-voo?

could you write it down for me, please?
você poderia escrever quanto é?
vo-seh poh-deh-ree-a eess-kreh-veH kwan-too eh?

can I pay by credit card?
posso pagar com cartão de crédito?
poss-oo pa-gaH koŋ kar-towŋ djee kreh-djee-too?

I'll pay in cash
vou pagar em dinheiro
voh pa-gar ayŋ djeen-yay-roo

I'm sorry, I haven't got any change
desculpe, mas não tenho dinheiro trocado
djeess-kool-pee, mass nowŋ ten-yoo djeen-yay-roo troh-kah-doo

can I have a receipt?
você pode me dar um recibo?
vo-seh po-djee mee dar oom Heh-see-boo?

Understanding

pagar no caixa
pay at the checkout

como deseja/vai pagar?
how would you like to pay?

tem menor?
do you have anything smaller?

assine aqui, por favor
sign here, please

você tem um documento de identificação?
have you got any ID?

FOOD

Expressing yourself

where can I buy food around here?
onde eu posso comprar comida aqui perto?
on-djee eh-oo poss-oo kom-praH koh-mee-da a-kee pair-too?

is there a market?
há algum mercado?
ah al-goom mair-kah-doo?

is there a bakery around here?
há alguma padaria por perto?
ah al-goo-ma pa-da-ree-a poor pair-too?

I'm looking for the cereal aisle
estou procurando cereais
eess-toh proh-koo-ran-doo seh-ree-ah-eess

I'd like five slices of ham
eu queria cinco fatias de presunto
eh-oo keh-ree-a seen-koo fa-tchee-ass djee preh-zoon-too

I'd like some goat's cheese
eu queria queijo de cabra
eh-oo keh-ree-a kay-Joo djee kah-bra

it's for four people
é para quatro pessoas
eh pah-ra kwah-troo pess-oh-ass

about 300 grams
cerca de trezentos gramas
sair-ka djee treh-zen-tooss grah-mass

a kilo of apples, please
um quilo de maçãs, por favor
oom kee-loo djee ma-sanss, poor fa-voH

a bit less/more
um pouco menos/mais
oom poh-koo meh-nooss/ma-eess

can I taste it?
posso provar?
poss-oo proh-vaH?

Understanding

caseiro/caseira   homemade
delicatessen   delicatessen

melhor consumir antes de …   best before …
especialidades regionais   local specialities
orgânico/orgânica   organic

há um mercado todas as manhãs até a uma
there's a market every morning until 1pm

há um armazém na esquina que fica aberto até tarde
there's a store just on the corner that's open late

CLOTHES

Expressing yourself

I'm looking for the menswear section
estou procurando a seção masculina
eess-toh proh-koo-ran-doo a seh-sown mass-koo-lee-na

no thanks, I'm just looking
não, obrigado *(m)*/obrigada *(f)*, estou só olhando
nown oh-bree-gah-doo/oh-bree-gah-da, eess-toh so ol-yan-doo

can I try it on?   **I take a size …** *(in shoes)*
posso experimentar?   calço …
poss-oo eess-peh-ree-men-taH?   *kal-soo …*

where are the changing rooms?
onde ficam os vestiários?
on-djee fee-kown ooss vess-tchee-ar-yooss?

it doesn't fit
não me serve
nown mee sair-vee

it's too big/small
é muito grande/pequeno *(m)*/pequena *(f)*
eh mween-too gran-djee/peh-keh-noo/peh-keh-na

do you have it in another colour?
tem outras cores?
tayn oh-trass koh-reess?

do you have it in a smaller/bigger size?
tem um número maior/menor?
*tayη oom **noo**-meh-roo ma-**yoH**/meh-**noH**?*

do you have them in red?
tem vermelho?
*tayη vair-**mel**-yoo?*

yes, that's fine, I'll take them
sim, está ótimo, vou levar
*seem, eess-**ta** o-tchee-moo, voh leh-**vaH***

no, I don't like it
não gosto
*nowη **goss**-too*

I'll think about it
vou pensar
*voh pen-**saH***

I'd like to return this, it doesn't fit
queria devolver isso, não serve
*keh-**ree**-a deh-vol-**vair** eess-oo, nowη **sair**-vee*

this ... has a hole in it, can I get a refund?
este/esta ... tem um buraco, posso devolver?
*ehss-tchee/ess-ta ... tayη oom boo-**rah**-koo, **poss**-oo deh-vol-**veH**?*

Understanding

aberto aos domingos	open Sundays
os artigos em liquidação não são trocados	sale items cannot be returned
roupa de criança	children's clothes
roupa de homem	menswear
roupa de mulher	ladieswear
vestiários	changing rooms

posso ajudar?
can I help you?

só temos em azul e preto
we only have it in blue or black

não temos nesse número/tamanho
we don't have any left in that size

fica bem em você
it suits you

te cai bem
it's a good fit

se não servir, pode devolver
you can bring it back if it doesn't fit

SOUVENIRS AND PRESENTS

Expressing yourself

I'm looking for a present to take home
estou procurando um presente para levar
eess-*toh* proh-koo-*ran*-doo oom preh-*zen*-tchee *pah*-ra leh-*vaH*

I'd like something that's easy to transport
eu queria alguma coisa fácil de transportar
eh-oo keh-*ree*-a al-*goo*-ma *koy*-za *fah*-seew djee tranz-por-*taH*

it's for a little girl of four
é para uma menina de quatro anos
eh *pah*-ra *oo*-ma meh-*nee*-na djee *kwah*-troo *ah*-nooss

could you gift-wrap it for me?
pode embrulhar? é para presente
po-djee em-brool-*yaH*? eh *pah*-ra preh-*zen*-tchee

Understanding

de madeira/prata/ouro/lã   made of wood/silver/gold/wool
feito à mão   handmade
produto artesanal   traditionally made product

quanto quer gastar?
how much do you want to spend?

é para presente?   **é típico/típica da região**
is it for a present?   it's typical of the region

PHOTOS

The basics

black and white	em preto e branco *ayη preh-too ee bran-koo*
camera	máquina fotográfica *mah-kee-na foh-toh-grah-fee-ka*, câmera (fotográfica) *kah-meh-ra (foh-toh-grah-fee-ka)*
colour	colorido *koh-loh-ree-doo*
copy	cópia *ko-pee-a*
digital camera	câmera digital *kah-meh-ra djee-Jee-tahw*, máquina digital *mah-kee-na djee-Jee-tahw*
exposure	exposição *eess-poh-zee-sowη*
film	filme (fotográfico) *feel-mee (foh-toh-grah-fee-koo)*
flash	flash *flesh-ee*
glossy	brilhante *breel-yan-tchee*, com brilho *koη breel-yoo*
matt	opaco *oh-pah-koo*, sem brilho *sayη breel-yoo*
memory card	cartão para máquina digital *kar-towη pah-ra mah-kee-na djee-Jee-tahw*
negative	negativo *neh-ga-tchee-voo*
passport photo	fotografia para passaporte *foh-toh-gra-fee-a pah-ra pass-a-por-tchee*
photo booth	cabine de fotografia automática *ka-bee-nee djee foh-toh-gra-fee-a ow-toh-mah-tchee-ka*
reprint	nova cópia *no-va ko-pee-a*
slide	eslaide *ee-sla-ee-djee*
to get photos developed	mandar revelar as fotografias *man-daH Heh-veh-laH ass foh-toh-gra-fee-ass*
to take a photo/photos	tirar/bater uma fotografia *tchee-rar/ba-tchair oo-ma foh-toh-gra-fee-a*

Expressing yourself

could you take a photo of us, please?
você poderia tirar uma fotografia nossa, por favor?
vo-seh poh-deh-ree-a tchee-rar oo-ma foh-toh-gra-fee-a noss-a, poor fa-voH?

you just have to press here/this button
basta apertar aqui/este botão
bass-ta a-pair-tar a-kee/ehss-tchee boh-town

I'd like a 200 ASA colour film
eu queria um filme colorido de ISO 200
eh-oo keh-ree-a oom feel-mee koh-loh-ree-doo djee ee-zoo doo-zen-tooss

do you have black and white films?
tem filmes para bater fotografias em preto e branco?
tayn feel-meess pah-ra ba-tcheH foh-toh-gra-fee-ass ayn preh-too ee bran-koo?

how much is it to develop a film of 36 photos?
quanto custa revelar um filme de trinta e seis poses?
kwan-too kooss-ta Heh-veh-lar oom feel-mee djee treen-ta ee sayss poh-zeess

I'd like to have this film developed
eu queria revelar este filme
eh-oo keh-ree-a Heh-veh-lar ehss-tchee feel-mee

I'd like extra copies of some of the photos
eu queria fazer cópias de algumas fotografias
eh-oo keh-ree-a fa-zeH ko-pee-ass djee al-goo-mass dass foh-toh-gra-fee-ass

three copies of this one and two of this one
três cópias desta aqui e duas desta
trehss ko-pee-ass dess-ta a-kee ee doo-ass dess-ta

can I print my digital photos here?
dá para imprimir as minhas fotografias (digitais) aqui?
da pah-ra eem-pree-meer ass meen-yass foh-toh-gra-fee-ass (djee-Jee-tah-eess) a-kee?

do you sell memory cards?
você vende cartões para máquinas digitais?
vo-seh ven-djee kar-toyŋss pah-ra mah-kee-nass djee-Jee-tah-eess?

can you put these photos on a CD for me?
você pode gravar essas fotografias em um CD para mim?
vo-seh po-djee gra-var ess-ass foh-toh-gra-fee-ass noom seh-deh pah-ra meeŋ?

I've come to pick up my photos
vim buscar as minhas fotografias
veen booss-kar ass meen-yass foh-toh-gra-fee-ass

I've got a problem with my camera
a minha máquina (fotográfica) está com problema
a meen-ya mah-kee-na (foh-toh-grah-fee-ka) eess-ta kon proh-bleh-ma

I don't know what it is
não sei o que é
nown say oo keh eh

the flash doesn't work
o flash não funciona
oo flesh-ee nown foon-see-oh-na

Understanding

formato normal	standard format
formato 10 por 15	4" x 6" format
fotografias em CD	photos on CD
revelação em uma hora	photos developed in one hour

talvez a pilha esteja fraca
maybe the battery's dead

temos uma máquina para imprimir fotografias digitais
we have a machine for printing digital photos

em nome de quem, por favor?
what's the name, please?

para quando você quer?
when do you want them for?

podemos revelar as fotos em uma hora
we can develop them in an hour

as fotos ficam prontas na quinta-feira ao partir do meio-dia
your photos will be ready on Thursday from noon

BANKS $

There are two government-owned banks in Brazil, Banco do Brasil and Caixa Econômica Federal. The major private banks are HSBC, Banco Itaú, Banespa, Bradesco, with foreign banks such as Citibank in the main cities. Look for the **câmbio** department.

Banks open between 10am and 4pm, but they can be quite slow and often cease transactions at 3pm. Try branches in major airports instead, if possible, as these stay open much longer and their rates are more favourable. It can also be quicker to use travel agencies and large hotels which also exchange traveller's cheques and foreign currency. Alternatively, there is a large network of ATMs for card transactions, but these can often have large queues.

Banks are closed at weekends and on public holidays. The US dollar is the most useful currency to take, being widely accepted. Try to keep your Brazilian currency in smaller bills, because large notes may be difficult to change in shops and restaurants.

The Brazilian currency is the **real** (plural **reais**), written R$, and small coins are multiples of the **centavo**. There are notes of 1, 2, 5, 10, 20, 50 and 100 reais (100-real notes are actually quite rare), and coins of 1, 5, 10, 25, 50 centavos and 1 real.

The basics

bank	banco *ban-koo*
bank account	conta bancária *kon-ta ban-kah-ree-a*
banknote	nota *no-ta*
bureau de change	casa de câmbio *kah-za djee kam-bee-oo*
cashpoint	caixa automático *ka-ee-sha ow-toh-mah-tchee-koo*
change	câmbio *kam-bee-oo*
cheque	cheque *sheh-kee*
coin	moeda *moh-eh-da*
commission	comissão *koh-mee-sowŋ*
credit card	cartão de crédito *kar-towŋ djee kreh-djee-too*

debit card	cartão de débito *kar-town djee deh-bee-too*
PIN (number)	senha *sen-ya*
transfer	transferência *tranz-feh-ren-see-a*
Travellers Cheques®	cheques de viagem *sheh-keess djee vee-ah-Jayn*
withdrawal	saque *sah-kee*
to change	trocar *troh-kaH*
to withdraw	sacar (dinheiro) *sa-kaH (djeen-yay-roo)*

Expressing yourself

where I can get some money changed?
onde eu posso trocar dinheiro?
on-djee eh-oo poss-oo troh-kaH djeen-yay-roo?

are banks open on Saturdays?
os bancos abrem aos sábados?
ooss ban-kooss ah-brayn owss sah-ba-dooss?

I'm looking for a cashpoint
estou procurando um caixa automático
eess-toh proh-koo-ran-doo oom ka-ee-sha ow-toh-mah-tchee-koo

I'd like to change £100
eu queria trocar cem libras
eh-oo keh-ree-a troh-kaH sayn lee-brass

what commission do you charge?
quanto é a comissão?
kwan-too eh a koh-mee-sown?

I'd like to transfer some money
eu queria transferir dinheiro
eh-oo keh-ree-a tranz-feh-reeH djeen-yay-roo

I'd like to report the loss of my credit card
eu gostaria de informar a perda do meu cartão de crédito
eh-oo goss-ta-ree-a djee een-for-mar a pair-da doo meh-oo kar-town djee kreh-djee-too

the cashpoint has swallowed my card
o caixa automático engoliu o meu cartão
oo ka-ee-sha ow-toh-mah-tchee-koo en-gol-yoo oo meh-oo kar-town

Understanding

insira o seu cartão
please insert your card

insira a sua senha
please enter your PIN number

selecione o valor do saque
please select amount for withdrawal

saque com comprovante
withdrawal with receipt

saque sem comprovante
withdrawal without receipt

fora de serviço
out of service

POST OFFICES

(i) A post office is called an **agência dos correios** and the main one can be found in most large town centres in a building called **Correios e Telégrafos** – there are usually other smaller ones which deal with only basic services. Signs and postboxes are coloured bright yellow.

Sending letters and cards abroad is relatively cheap, whereas parcels are rather expensive. You will find separate post boxes for national and international mail. Buying stamps is similarly divided into internal and foreign rates – try to find a queue where a franking machine service is provided since it will move much faster! Delivery to Europe and the US by airmail can take a week, but surface mail will take much longer – you can speed things up by asking for **prioritário** and for even safer delivery there is registered mail (**carta registrada**).

Post offices are generally open from 8am to 6pm Monday to Friday, and Saturday from 8am to midday.

The basics

address	endereço *en-deh-reh-soo*
airmail	correio aéreo *koh-Hay-oo a-air-yoo*
envelope	envelope *en-veh-loh-pee*
letter	carta *kar-ta*
mail	correio *koh-Hay-oo*
parcel	encomenda *en-koh-men-da*, pacote *pa-koh-tchee*
post	correio *koh-Hay-oo*
postbox	caixa do correio *ka-ee-sha doo koh-Hay-oo*
postcard	(cartão-)postal *(kar-towη-)poss-tahw*
postcode	código postal *ko-djee-goo poss-tahw*, CEP *seh-pee*
post office	(agência dos) correios *(a-Jenss-ya dooss) koh-Hay-ooss*
stamp	selo *seh-loo*
to post	pôr no correio *pohr noo koh-Hay-oo*
to send	enviar *en-vee-aH*

Expressing yourself

is there a post office around here?
tem alguma agência dos correios aqui perto?
tayŋ al-goo-ma a-Jen-see-a dooss koh-Hay-ooss a-kee pair-too?

is there a postbox near here?
tem alguma caixa do correio aqui perto?
tayŋ al-goo-ma ka-ee-sha doo koh-Hay-oo a-kee pair-too?

is the post office open on Saturdays?
o correio abre aos sábados?
oo koh-Hay-oo ah-bree ah-ooss sah-ba-dooss?

what time does the post office close?
a que horas fecha o correio?
a keh oh-rass feh-sha oo koh-Hay-oo?

do you sell stamps?
você vende selos?
vo-seh ven-djee seh-looss?

I'd like … stamps for the UK, please
eu queria … selos para o Reino Unido, por favor
eh-oo keh-ree-a … seh-looss pah-ra oo Hay-noo oo-nee-doo, poor fa-voH

how much is a stamp to Scotland?
quanto custa um selo para a Escócia?
kwan-too kooss-ta oom seh-loo pah-ra a eess-koh-see-a?

how much would it be to send this/this package?
quanto custa enviar isso/esse pacote?
kwan-too kooss-ta en-vee-ar ee-soo/eh-see pa-koh-tchee?

how long will it take to arrive?
quanto tempo demora para chegar?
kwan-too tem-poo deh-moh-ra pah-ra sheh-gaH?

where can I buy envelopes?
onde posso comprar envelopes?
on-djee poss-oo kom-prar en-veh-loh-peess?

is there any post for me?
tem carta para mim?
tayŋ kar-ta pah-ra meeŋ?

Understanding

carta registrada	recorded letter
carteiro	postman
destinatário	addressee
frágil	handle with care/fragile
porte	postage
primeira coleta	first collection
remetente	sender
tarifa postal	postage
última coleta	last collection

para comprar selos, é no guichê ao lado
for stamps go to the next counter

quer enviar por correio simples ou prioritário?
do you want to sent it by normal post or fast service?

leva/demora de três a cinco dias
it'll take between three and five days

fica em 10 reais
it will cost you 10 reals

Understanding addresses

Common abbreviations:

A/C	= aos cuidados de	care of
Av.	= avenida	avenue
Dt.º	= direito	right
Esq.º	= esquerdo	left
Pr.	= praça	square
R.	= rua	street

House numbers are written after the name of the street. An interesting feature of this number is that it also tells you how many metres the house is from the beginning of the street – very useful for knowing how far you have to walk if it is a long road!

INTERNET CAFÉS AND E-MAIL | WWW

You will find internet cafés (**cibercafés**) in most regions of Brazil, including many villages and out-of-the-way places! The Brazilians have an extensive network and have taken to the technology more than most other countries. It is one of the best ways in this vast country of finding out information and contacting people, and you will find we have added a number of useful sites to the reference section at the end of this book.

The basics

at sign (@)	arroba *a-**Hoh**-ba*
e-mail	correio eletrônico *koh-**Hay**-oo eh-leh-**troh**-nee-koo*, e-mail *ee-**mail***
e-mail address	e-mail *ee-**mail***
file	arquivo *ar-**kee**-voo*
Internet café	cibercafé *see-ber-ka-**feh***
key	tecla *teh-kla*
keyboard	teclado *teh-**klah**-doo*
new	novo *no-voo*
to close	fechar *feh-**shaH***
to copy	copiar *koh-pee-**aH***
to cut	recortar *Heh-kor-**taH***
to delete	apagar *a-pa-**gaH***
to download	baixar *by-**shaH***, fazer o download de *fa-**zair** oo download djee*
to e-mail somebody	enviar um e-mail a alguém *en-vee-**ar** oom ee-**mail** a al-**gayŋ***
to exit	sair *sa-**eeH***
to open	abrir *a-**breeH***
to paste	colar *koh-**laH***
to print	imprimir *eem-pree-**meeH***
to receive	receber *Heh-seh-**beH***

to save	salvar *sal-vaH*
to search	pesquisar *pess-kee-zaH*, buscar *booss-kaH*
to send an e-mail	enviar um e-mail *en-vee-ar oom ee-mail*

Expressing yourself

is there an Internet café near here?
há algum café com Internet aqui perto?
ah al-goom ka-feh koŋ een-tair-neh-tchee a-kee pair-too?

do you have an e-mail address?
você tem e-mail?
vo-seh tayŋ ee-mail?

my e-mail address is david_768@o-net.com
o meu e-mail é david_768@o-net.com
oo meh-oo ee-mail eh da-veed soob-leen-yah-doo seh-tchee sayss oy-too a-Hoh-ba oh trah-soo neh-tchee pon-too kom

how do I get online?
como eu me conecto à Internet?
koh-moo eh-oo mee koh-nek-too ah een-tair-neh-tchee?

I'd just like to check my e-mail
só queria verificar o meu e-mail
so keh-ree-a veh-ree-fee-kar oo meh-oo ee-mail

would you mind helping me, I'm not sure what to do
você me pode ajudar, não sei exatamente o que preciso fazer
vo-seh mee po-djee a-Joo-daH, nowŋ say ee-zah-ta-men-tchee oo keh preh-see-zoo fa-zeH

I can't find the at sign on this keyboard
não encontro a arroba neste teclado
nowŋ en-kon-troo a a-Hoh-ba ness-tchee teh-klah-doo

it's not working
não está funcionando
nowŋ eess-ta foon-see-oh-nan-doo

there's something wrong with the computer, it's frozen
tem alguma coisa errada com o computador, travou
tayŋ al-goo-ma koy-za eh-Hah-da koŋ oo kom-poo-ta-doH, tra-voh

how much will it be for half an hour?
quanto custa meia hora?
kwan-too kooss-ta may-a oh-ra?

when do I pay?
quando é que eu pago?
kwan-doo eh keh eh-oo pah-goo?

Understanding

caixa de entrada	inbox
caixa de saída	outbox

precisa esperar uns 20 minutos
you'll have to wait for 20 minutes or so

se precisar de mim, é só chamar
I'm here if you need me

pergunte se você não souber o que fazer
just ask if you're not sure what to do

basta inserir esta senha para fazer logon
just enter this password to log on

Telephone numbers are usually given one digit at a time in Portuguese, as in English, although there are no hard and fast rules – you can also say the number in groups of two digits, ie sixteen, twenty-five, etc. Note that zero is pronounced "**zeh**-roo" and, instead of the number 6, Brazilians use the word **meia** (pronounced "**may**-a") – this is to avoid confusion between 3 and 6 which have rather similar sounds

Phone booths can be found nearly everywhere (called **orelhão** – "big ear" – because of their round shape) and require a phone card (**cartão telefônico**). These cost from R$20 and are available from cafés, newspaper kiosks and street vendors.

International calls are relatively expensive, so try to call between 8pm and 5am as there is a 25 per cent discount (but remember the time difference back home!). Roaming service is available for mobiles, but coverage can vary a lot.

To call Brazil from the UK/US: dial 00 + 55 + 2-digit area code + 8-digit number (numbers beginning 2 – 6 are land lines, numbers beginning 7 – 9 are mobiles).

To call the UK from Brazil you will first have to decide which international carrier code to use (21 for Embratel, 23 for Intelig), then dial 00 + carrier code + 44 + area code (minus the first 0) + number. The US is similar, ie 00 + carrier code + 1 and then the usual US codes.

The basics

answering machine	secretária eletrônica *seh-kreh-**tar**-ee-a eh-leh-**troh**-nee-ka*
call	ligação *lee-ga-**sowη***
directory enquiries	informações *een-for-ma-**soyηss***
hello	*(on phone)* alô *a-**loh***
international call	ligação internacional *lee-ga-**sowη** een-tair-nass-yoh-**now***
local call	ligação local *lee-ga-**sowη** loh-**kow***
message	mensagem *men-**sah**-Jayη*

mobile	(telefone) celular *(teh-leh-foh-nee) seh-loo-laH*
national call	ligação nacional *lee-ga-sown nass-yoh-now*
phone	telefone *teh-leh-foh-nee*
phone book	lista telefônica *leess-ta teh-leh-foh-nee-ka*
phone box	cabine telefônica *ka-bee-nee teh-leh-foh-nee-ka*
phone call	ligação *lee-ga-sown*, telefonema *teh-leh-foh-neh-ma*
phone number	número de telefone *noo-meh-roo djee teh-leh-foh-nee*
phonecard	cartão telefônico *kar-town teh-leh-foh-nee-koo*
ringtone	(sinal de) linha *(see-now djee) leen-ya*
telephone	telefone *teh-leh-foh-nee*
top-up card	cartão para celular *kar-town pah-ra seh-loo-laH*
Yellow Pages®	Páginas Amarelas® *pah-Jee-nass a-ma-reh-lass*
to call someone	ligar para alguém *lee-gar pah-ra al-gayŋ*

Expressing yourself

where can I buy a phonecard?
onde eu posso comprar um cartão telefônico?
on-djee eh-oo poss-oo kom-prar oom kar-towŋ teh-leh-foh-nee-koo?

a ... -reals top-up card, please
eu queria um cartão de ... reais para o meu celular, por favor
eh-oo keh-ree-a oom kar-towŋ djee ... Hee-ah-eess pah-ra oo meh-oo seh-loo-laH, poor fa-voH

I'd like to make a reverse-charge call
eu queria fazer uma ligação a cobrar
eh-oo keh-ree-a fa-zair oo-ma lee-ga-sowŋ a koh-braH

is there a phone box near here, please?
sabe se tem alguma cabine telefônica aqui perto?
sah-bee see tayŋ al-goo-ma ka-bee-nee teh-leh-foh-nee-ka a-kee pair-too?

can I plug my phone in here to recharge it?
posso recarregar o meu celular aqui?
poss-oo Heh-ka-Heh-gar oo meh-oo seh-loo-lar a-kee?

do you have a mobile number?
tem celular?
tayŋ seh-loo-laH?

TELEPHONE

103

where can I contact you?
como eu posso entrar em contato com ele?
ko-moo eh-oo poss-oo en-trar ayη kon-ta-too koη eh-lee?

did you get my message?
recebeu a minha mensagem?
Heh-seh-beh-oo a meen-ya men-sah-Jayη?

Understanding

o número que você digitou não foi reconhecido
the number you have dialled has not been recognized

pressione a tecla sustenido
please press the hash key

MAKING A CALL

Expressing yourself

hello, this is David Brown (speaking)
alô? aqui é David Brown
a-loh? a-kee eh david brown

hello? could I speak to ..., please?
alô? eu poderia falar com ..., por favor?
a-loh, eh-oo poh-deh-ree-a fa-laH koη ..., poor fa-voH?

hello, is that Isabel?
alô? é a Isabel?
a-loh? eh a ee-za-behw?

do you speak English?
você fala inglês?
vo-seh fah-la een-glehss?

I'd like to speak to ...
gostaria de falar com ...
goss-ta-ree-a djee fa-laH koη ...

could you speak more slowly, please?
você poderia falar mais devagar, por favor?
vo-seh poh-deh-ree-a fa-laH ma-eess djee-va-gaH, poor fa-voH?

I can't hear you, could you speak up?
não consigo ouvir, daria para falar mais alto?
nowŋ kon-see-goo oh-veeH, da-ree-a pah-ra fa-laH ma-eess al-too?

could you tell him/her I called?
você poderia dizer para ele/ela que eu liguei?
vo-seh poh-deh-ree-a djee-zeH pah-ra eh-lee/ell-a keh eh-oo lee-gay?

could you ask him/her to call me back?
você poderia pedir para ele me ligar?
vo-seh poh-deh-ree-a peh-djeeH pah-ra eh-lee mee lee-gaH?

I'll call back later
eu ligo mais tarde
eh-oo lee-goo ma-eess tar-djee

my name is … and my number is …
o meu nome é … e o meu número é …
oo meh-oo no-mee eh … ee oo meh-oo noo-meh-roo eh …

do you know when he/she might be available?
quando é que eu posso falar com ele/ela?
kwan-doo eh keh eh-oo poss-oo fa-laH koŋ eh-lee/ell-a?

thank you, goodbye
obrigado *(m)*/obrigada *(f)*, tchau
oo-bree-gah-doo/oo-bree-gah-da, tchow

Understanding

quem fala?
who's calling?

de onde fala?
what number is that?

você discou o número errado
you've dialled the wrong number

desculpe, foi engano
sorry, I've dialled the wrong number

ele/ela não está
he's/she's not here at the moment

quer deixar recado?
do you want to leave a message?

eu digo para ele/ela que você ligou
I'll tell him/her you called

eu peço para ele/ela ligar
I'll ask him/her to call you back

vou passar para ele/ela
I'll just hand you over to him/her

aguarde um momento
hold on

PROBLEMS

Expressing yourself

I don't know the code
não sei qual é o código
*nowɲ say kwal eh oo **ko**-djee-goo*

it's engaged
dá sinal de ocupado
*da see-**now** djee oh-koo-**pah**-doo*

there's no reply
ninguém atende
*neen-**gayɲ** a-**ten**-djee*

I couldn't get through
não consegui ligar
*nowɲ kon-seh-**ghee** lee-**gaH***

I don't have much credit left on my phone
estou quase sem crédito no meu celular
*eess-**toh** kwah-zee sayɲ **kreh**-djee-too noo **meh**-oo seh-loo-**laH***

we're about to get cut off
vão cortar o telefone
*vowɲ kor-**tar** oo teh-leh-**foh**-nee*

I can't get a signal
estou sem linha
*eess-**toh** sayɲ **leen**-ya*

the reception's really bad
a recepção é muito ruim aqui
*a heh-sep-**sowɲ** eh mweeɲ-too Hoo-**eeɲ** a-**kee***

Understanding

estou ouvindo muito mal
I can hardly hear you

a ligação é péssima
it's a bad line

Some informal expressions

fazer uma ligação to make a call
desligar o telefone na cara de alguém to hang up on someone

HEALTH

Although Brazil has excellent private medical and dental care facilities, make sure you are properly insured before travelling, as you will need to pay for both minor illness costs and major hospital bills. You may be required to be vaccinated against certain diseases (such as yellow fever, cholera or malaria, amongst others) if you are travelling to the central or tropical regions – best to check with your own government health authorities before travelling, since regulations can often change.

On the whole, you should not have problems in Brazil as long as you take the necessary precautions: when not in town, aim to drink from cans and bottles rather than tap water.

Pharmacies open during normal shopping hours, but there will always be one giving 24-hour local cover, details of which are shown on all their doors. You can obtain medicines from **farmácias** (chemists) and **drogarias** (drug stores).

The emergency number for the ambulance service is 192.

The basics

allergy	alergia *a-lair-Jee-a*
ambulance	ambulância *am-boo-lan-see-a*
aspirin	aspirina *ass-pee-ree-na*
blister	bolha (de água) *bol-ya (djee ah-gwa)*
blood	sangue *san-ghee*
broken	quebrado/quebrada *keh-brah-doo/keh-brah-da*
burn	queimadura *kay-ma-doo-ra*
casualty (department)	emergência *ee-mer-Jen-see-a*
chemist's	farmácia *far-mah-see-a*
cold	gripe *gree-pee*
condom	preservativo *preh-zair-va-tchee-voo*
constipation	prisão de ventre *pree-zown djee ven-tree*
cough	tosse *toh-see*
dentist	dentista *den-tcheess-ta*
diarrhoea	diarréia *djee-a-Hay-a*

doctor	médico *meh-djee-koo*
flu	gripe *gree-pee*
food poisoning	intoxicação alimentar *een-tok-see-ka-sown a-lee-men-taH*
GP	clínico geral *klee-nee-koo Jeh-rahw*
gynaecologist	ginecologista *Jee-neh-koh-loh-Jeess-ta*
hospital	hospital *oss-pee-tahw*
infection	infecção *een-fek-sown*
medicine	medicamento *meh-djee-ka-men-too*
painkiller	analgésico *a-nal-Jeh-zee-koo*
period	menstruação *menss-troo-a-sown*
plaster	Band-Aid® *ban-day-djee*
rash	irritação de pele *ee-Hee-ta-sown djee peh-lee*
spot	espinha *eess-peen-ya*
sunburn	queimadura do sol *kay-ma-doo-ra doo sow*
sunstroke	insolação *een-soh-la-sown*
surgical spirit	álcool etílico *al-kwol eh-tchee-lee-koo*
tablet	comprimido *kom-pree-mee-doo*
temperature *(fever)*	febre *feh-bree*
vaccination	vacina *va-see-na*
x-ray	raio X *Hy-oo sheess*
to cough	tossir *toh-seeH*
to disinfect	desinfetar *djeez-een-feh-taH*
to faint	desmaiar *djeeJ-ma-yaH*
to vomit	vomitar *voh-mee-taH*

Expressing yourself

does anyone have an aspirin/a tampon/a plaster, by any chance?
por acaso alguém não tem uma aspirina/um absorvente/um Band-Aid®?
poor a-kah-zoo al-gayn nown tayn oo-ma ass-pee-ree-na/oom ab-sor-ven-tchee/oom ban-day-djee?

I need to see a doctor
preciso ver um médico
preh-see-zoo vair oom meh-djee-koo

where can I find a doctor?
onde posso encontrar um médico?
on-djee poss-oo en-kon-trar oom meh-djee-koo?

I'd like to make an appointment for today
eu queria marcar uma consulta para hoje
*eh-oo keh-**ree**-a mar-**kar** oo-ma kon-**sool**-ta **pah**-ra oh-Jee*

as soon as possible
o mais cedo possível
*oo ma-eess **seh**-doo poh-**see**-vehw*

no, it doesn't matter
não, não importa
*nown, nown eem-**por**-ta*

can you send an ambulance to …?
você pode mandar uma ambulância para …?
*vo-**seh** po-djee man-**dar** oo-ma am-boo-**lan**-see-a **pah**-ra …?*

I've broken my glasses
quebrei os óculos
*keh-**bray** ooz o-koo-looss*

I've lost a contact lens
perdi uma lente de contato
*pair-**djee** oo-ma **len**-tchee djee kon-**tah**-too*

HEALTH

Understanding

consultório médico	doctor's surgery
farmácia 24 horas	duty pharmacy
horário de atendimento	surgery hours
receita	prescription
sala de espera	waiting room
emergência	casualty department

não temos nenhum horário até quinta-feira
there are no available appointments until Thursday

pode ser sexta-feira às duas horas?
is Friday at 2pm OK?

AT THE DOCTOR'S OR THE HOSPITAL

Expressing yourself

I have an appointment with Dr …
tenho consulta marcada com o Dr. …
*ten-yoo kon-**sool**-ta mar-**kah**-da kon oo doh-**toH**…*

I don't feel very well
não me sinto bem
*nowŋ mee **seen**-too bayŋ*

I feel very weak
me sinto muito fraco *(m)*/fraca *(f)*
*mee **seen**-too mweeŋ-too **frah**-koo/**frah**-ka*

I don't know what it is
não sei o que é
nowŋ say oo keh eh

I've been bitten/stung by …
fui mordido/picado por …
*fwee mor-**djee**-doo/pee-**kah**-doo poor …*

I've got a headache/toothache/stomachache/sore throat
estou com dor de cabeça/dente/estômago/garganta
*eess-**toh** koŋ doH djee ka-**beh**-sa/**den**-tchee/eess-**toh**-ma-goo/gar-**gan**-ta*

my back hurts
me doem as costas
*mee **doh**-ayŋ ass **koss**-tass*

it hurts
dói
doy

it hurts here
dói aqui
doy a-kee

I feel sick
estou enjoado *(m)*/enjoada *(f)*
*eess-**toh** en-Joh-**ah**-doo/en-Joh-**ah**-da*

it's got worse
piorou
*pee-oh-**roh***

it's been three days
faz três dias
fass trehss djee-ass

it started last night
começou ontem à noite
*koh-meh-**soh** on-tayŋ ah **noy**-tchee*

I've got a temperature
estou com febre
*eess-**toh** koŋ **feh**-bree*

it's never happened to me before
nunca me aconteceu
*nooŋ-ka mee a-kon-teh-**seh**-oo*

I have asthma
tenho asma
*ten-yoo **az**-ma*

I have a heart condition
sofro do coração
*soh-froo doo koh-ra-**sowŋ***

I've been on antibiotics for a week and I'm not getting any better
estou tomando antibióticos há uma semana e não estou me sentindo
melhor
*eess-**toh** toh-**man**-doo an-tchee-bee-**o**-tchee-kooss ah **oo**-ma seh-**mah**-na ee
nowŋ eess-**toh** mee sen-**tcheen**-doo mel-**yoH***

it itches
coça
koh-sa

I'm … months pregnant
estou grávida de … meses
*eess-**toh** grah-**vee**-da djee … **meh**-zeess*

I'm on the pill/minipill
tomo anticoncepcional/micro-pílula
toh-moo an-tchee-kon-sep-see-oh-now/mee-kroh-pee-loo-la

I'm allergic to penicillin
sou alérgico *(m)*/alérgica *(f)* à penicilina
soh a-lair-Jee-koo/a-lair-Jee-ka ah peh-nee-see-lee-na

I've twisted my ankle
torci o pé
tor-see oo peh

I fell and hurt my back
caí e machuquei as costas
ka-ee ee ma-shoo-kay ass koss-tass

I've had a blackout
perdi os sentidos
pair-djee ooss sen-tchee-dooss

I've lost a filling
perdi uma obturação
pair-djee oo-ma ob-too-ra-sowɲ

is it serious?
é grave?
eh grah-vee?

is it contagious?
é contagioso?
eh kon-ta-Jee-oh-zoo?

how is he/she?
como é que ele/ela está?
koh-moo eh keh eh-lee/ell-a eess-ta?

how much do I owe you?
quanto devo?
kwan-too deh-voo?

can I have a receipt?
pode me dar um recibo?
po-djee mee dar oom Heh-see-boo?

Understanding

aguarde na sala de espera, por favor
please take a seat in the waiting room

onde é que dói?
where does it hurt?

respire fundo
take a deep breath

deite-se, por favor
lie down, please

dói quando eu aperto aqui?
does it hurt when I press here?

está vacinado/vacinada contra …?
have you been vaccinated against …?

é alérgico/alérgica a …?
are you allergic to …?

está tomando algum outro medicamento?
are you taking any other medication?

vou lhe dar uma receita
I'm going to write you a prescription

deve passar em alguns dias   **deve cicatrizar rapidamente**
it should clear up in a few days   it should heal quickly

vai ter que operar
you're going to need an operation

você vai precisar fazer exame de sangue
you'll need to have some blood tests done

volte em uma semana
come back and see me in a week

AT THE CHEMIST'S

Expressing yourself

I'd like a box of plasters, please
eu queria uma caixa de Band-Aid®, por favor
*eh-oo keh-**ree**-a oo-ma ka-ee-sha djee ban-**day**-djee, poor fa-**voH***

could I have something for a bad cold?
você teria alguma coisa para resfriado?
*vo-**seh** teh-**ree**-a al-**goo**-ma koy-za pah-ra Hess-free-**ah**-do?*

I need something for a cough
eu queria alguma coisa para a tosse
*eh-oo keh-**ree**-a al-**goo**-ma koy-za pah-ra a **toh**-see*

I'm allergic to aspirin
sou alérgico *(m)*/alérgica *(f)* à aspirina
*soh a-**lair**-Jee-koo/a-**lair**-Jee-ka ah ass-pee-**ree**-na*

I need the morning-after pill
preciso da pílula do dia seguinte
*preh-**see**-zoo da **pee**-loo-la doo **djee**-a seh-**geen**-tchee*

I'd like to try a homeopathic remedy
gostaria de tentar um remédio homeopático
*goss-ta-**ree**-a djee ten-**tar** oom Heh-**meh**-djee-oo oh-mee-oh-**pah**-tchee-koo*

Understanding

antiinflamatório	anti-inflammatory
aplicar	apply
cápsula	capsule
contra-indicações	contra-indications
creme	cream
drágea	tablet
para uso externo	for external use only
pastilha para a garganta	throat lozenge
pó	powder
pomada	ointment
possíveis efeitos colaterais	possible side effects
só com receita (médica)	available on prescription only
supositório	suppository
tomar três vezes ao dia antes das refeições	take three times a day before meals
xarope	syrup

HEALTH

> **Some informal expressions**
> **estar de molho** to be stuck in bed
> **estar acamado/acamada** to feel poorly
> **ter um desmaio** to pass out
> **estar abatido/a** to feel quite rough

PROBLEMS AND EMERGENCIES

The emergency numbers are 190 for the police, 192 for an ambulance and 193 for the fire brigade.

Brazil is generally just as safe as anywhere else. As in most cities, especially in poorer districts or near transport hubs, there are the inevitable thieves and muggers, so take normal precautions: try not to be conspicuous or carry expensive items, and don't walk alone at night. In the two large cities of Rio and São Paulo there have been outbreaks of violence in some districts from time to time, so pay particular attention to what the situation is like when you go – your embassy will have the latest details. If you enter Brazil without a visa and want to stay for more than 90 days, you will need to see the Federal Police.

The basics

accident	acidente *a-see-den-tchee*
ambulance	ambulância *am-boo-lan-see-a*
broken	quebrado/quebrada *keh-brah-doo/keh-brah-da*
coastguard	guarda-costeira *gwar-da koss-tay-ra*
disabled	deficiente *deh-fee-see-en-tchee*
doctor	médico/médica *meh-djee-koo/meh-djee-ka*
emergency	emergência *ee-mer-Jen-see-a*
fire brigade	bombeiros *bom-bay-rooss*
fire	incêndio *een-sen-dee-oo*, fogo *foh-goo*
hospital	hospital *oss-pee-tow*
ill	doente *doo-en-tchee*
injured	ferido/ferida *feh-ree-doo/feh-ree-da*
police	polícia *poh-lee-see-a*

Expressing yourself

can you help me?
você me pode ajudar?
*vo-**seh** mee **po**-djee a-Joo-**daH**?*

help!
socorro!
*soh-**ko**-Hoo!*

fire!
fogo!
foh-goo!

be careful!
cuidado!
*kwee-**dah**-doo!*

it's an emergency!
é uma emergência!
*eh **oo**-ma ee-mer-**Jen**-see-a!*

there's been an accident
houve um acidente
*oh-vee oom a-see-**den**-tchee*

could I borrow your phone, please?
posso utilizar o seu telefone, por favor?
***poss**-oo oo-tee-lee-**zar** oo **seh**-oo teh-leh-**foh**-nee, poor fa-**voH**?*

I need a doctor, quick!
preciso de um médico, depressa!
*preh-**see**-zoo djee oom **meh**-djee-koo, deh-**press**-a!*

does anyone here speak English?
alguém fala inglês?
*al-**gayŋ fah**-la een-**gless**?*

I need to contact the British consulate
preciso entrar em contato com o consulado britânico
*preh-**see**-zoo en-**trar** ayŋ kon-**ta**-too koŋ oo kon-soo-**lah**-doo bree-**tah**-nee-koo*

where's the nearest police station?
onde fica a delegacia mais próxima?
*on-djee **fee**-ka a deh-leh-ga-**see**-a **ma**-eess **pross**-ee-ma?*

what do I have to do?
o que é que tenho que fazer?
*oo keh eh keh **ten**-yoo keh fa-**zeH**?*

my passport/credit card has been stolen
o meu passaporte/cartão de crédito foi roubado
*oo **meh**-oo pass-a-**por**-tchee/kar-**towŋ** djee **kreh**-djee-too foy Hoh-**bah**-doo*

my bag's been snatched
roubaram a minha carteira
Hoh-bah-rowη a meen-ya kar-tay-ra

I've lost …
perdi …
pair-djee …

I've been attacked
fui atacado (m)/atacada (f)
fwee a-ta-kah-doo/a-ta-kah-da

my son/daughter is missing
o meu filho/a minha filha desapareceu
oo meh-oo feel-yoo/a meen-ya feel-ya djee-za-pa-reh-seh-oo

my car's been towed away
o meu carro foi rebocado
oo meh-oo ka-Hoo foy Heh-boh-kah-doo

I've broken down
o meu carro pifou
oo meh-oo ka-Hoo pee-foh

my car's been broken into
arrombaram o meu carro
a-Hom-bah-rowη oo meh-oo ka-Hoo

there's a man following me
há um homem me seguindo
ah oom oh-mayη mee seh-geen-doo

is there disabled access?
há algum acesso especial para deficientes?
ah al-goom a-sess-oo eess-peh-see-ow pah-ra djee-fee-see-en-tcheess?

can you keep an eye on my things for a minute?
você se importa de dar uma olhada nas minhas coisas por um minuto?
vo-seh see eem-por-ta djee dar oo-ma ol-yaH-da nass meen-yass koy-zass poor oom mee-noo-too?

he's drowning, get help!
ele está se afogando, peçam ajuda!
eh-lee eess-ta see a-foh-gan-doo, pess-owη a-Joo-da!

she's not feeling well, please call a doctor/an ambulance
ela não está se sentindo bem, chamem um médico/a ambulância
ell-a nowη ees-ta see sen-tcheen-doo bayη, shah-mayη oom meh-djee-ko/a am-boo-lan-see-a

Understanding

achados e perdidos	lost property
caixa de primeiros-socorros	first aid box
cuidado com o cão	beware of the dog
farmácia 24 horas	duty pharmacy
pronto-socorro	ambulance/emergency service
quebrado/quebrada	out of order
saída de emergência	emergency exit
serviço de emergência	emergency services
serviço de reboque	breakdown service

POLICE

Expressing yourself

I want to report something stolen
eu queria dar parte de um roubo
eh-oo keh-ree-a a dar par-tchee djee oom Hoh-boo

I need a document from the police for my insurance company
eu preciso de um boletim de ocorrência da polícia para apresentar
para a companhia de seguros
*eh-oo preh-see-zoo djee oom boh-leh-tcheeη djee oh-koo-Hen-see-a da
poh-lee-see-a pah-ra a-preh-zen-taH pah-ra a kom-pan-yee-a djee seh-
goo-rooss*

Understanding

Filling in forms

sobrenome	surname
nome (de batismo)	first name
endereço	address
CEP	postcode
país	country
naturalidade	place of birth

estado civil	marital status
nacionalidade	nationality
data de nascimento	date of birth
local de nascimento	place of birth
idade	age
sexo	sex
duração da estadia	duration of stay
data de chegada/partida	arrival/departure date
profissão	occupation
número do passaporte	passport number

precisa pagar um imposto alfandegário por este artigo
there's customs duty to pay on this item

você se importaria de abrir a sacola?
would you open this bag, please?

o que está faltando?
what's missing?

quando é que aconteceu?
when did this happen?

onde você está hospedado?
where are you staying?

você pode descrevê-lo/descrevê-la?
can you describe him/her/it?

poderia preencher esta ficha?
would you fill in this form, please?

pode assinar aqui?
would you sign here, please?

Some informal expressions

cadeia prison
ir parar atrás das grades to go to prison/to get arrested
meter-se em encrencas to get into trouble

The basics

after	depois *deh-poyss*
already	já *Jah*
always	sempre *sem-pree*
at lunchtime	na hora do almoço *na oh-ra doo al-moh-soo*
at the beginning/end of	no início/no fim de *noo ee-nee-see-oo/noo feen djee*
at the moment	neste momento *ness-tchee moh-men-too*
before	antes *an-tcheess*
between ... and ...	entre as ... e as ... *en-tree ass ... ee ass ...*
day	dia *djee-a*
during	durante *doo-ran-tchee*
early	cedo *seh-doo*, adiantado/adiantada *a-djee-an-tah-doo/a-djee-an-tah-da*
evening	noite *noy-tchee*
for a long time	durante muito tempo *doo-ran-tchee mween-too tem-poo*
from ... to ...	de ... a ... *djee ... a ...*
from time to time	de vez em quando *djee vehz ayŋ kwan-doo*
in a little while	daqui a pouco *da-kee a poh-koo*
in the evening	à noite *ah noy-tchee*
in the middle of	no meio de *noo may-oo djee*
last	último/última *ool-tchee-moo/ool-tchee-ma*
late	tarde *tar-djee*, atrasado/atrasada *a-tra-zah-doo/a-tra-zah-da*
midday	meio-dia *may-oo djee-a*
midnight	meia-noite *may-a noy-tchee*
morning	manhã *man-yaŋ*
month	mês *mehss*
never	nunca *nooŋ-ka*
next	próximo/próxima *pross-ee-moo/pross-ee-ma*
night	noite *noy-tchee*
not yet	ainda não *a-een-da nowŋ*

now	agora *a-goh-ra*
occasionally	às vezes *ass veh-zeess*
often	muitas vezes *mweeη-tass veh-zeess*
rarely	raras vezes *Hah-rass veh-zeess*
recently	recentemente *Hess-en-tchee-men-tchee*
since	desde *dez-djee*
sometimes	algumas vezes *al-goo-mass veh-zeess*
soon	em breve *ayη breh-vee*
still	ainda *a-een-da*
straightaway	imediatamente *ee-meh-djee-ah-ta-men-tchee*
until	até *a-teh*
week	semana *seh-mah-na*
weekend	fim de semana *feeη djee seh-mah-na*
year	ano *ah-noo*

Expressing yourself

see you soon!
até mais!
a-teh ma-eess!

see you later!
até mais tarde!
a-teh ma-eess tar-djee!

see you on Monday!
até segunda!
a-teh seh-goon-da!

have a good weekend!
bom fim de semana!
boη feeη djee seh-mah-na!

sorry I'm late
desculpe a demora
dess-kool-pee a deh-moh-ra

I haven't been there yet
ainda não fui lá
a-een-da nowη fwee la

I haven't had time to ...
não tive tempo de ...
nowη tchee-vee tem-poo djee ...

I've got plenty of time
tenho muito tempo
ten-yoo mweeη-too tem-poo

I'm in a rush
estou com pressa
eess-toh koη press-a

hurry up!
depressa!
deh-press-a!

just a minute, please
espere um minuto, por favor
eess-peh-ree oom mee-noo-too, poor fa-voH

I had a late night
fui deitar tarde
fwee day-taH tar-djee

I got up very early
me levantei muito cedo
mee leh-van-tay mween-too seh-doo

I waited ages
fiquei horas esperando
fee-kay oh-raz eess-peh-ran-doo

I have to get up very early tomorrow to catch my plane
tenho que me levantar muito cedo para pegar o avião
ten-yoo keh mee leh-van-taH mween-too seh-doo pah-ra peh-gar oo a-vee-own

we only have four days left
só temos mais quatro dias
so teh-mooss ma-eess kwah-troo djee-ass

THE DATE

How to express dates

2 January 2008	**2 de janeiro de 2008**
in June 2008	**em junho de 2008**
from 2007 to 2008	**de 2007 a 2008**
100 BC	**no século I (um) antes de Cristo (a. C.)**
AD 300	**no século III (três) depois de Cristo (d. C.)**
nineteenth-century art	**a arte do século XIX (dezenove)**

The basics

... ago	... atrás *... a-trass*
in the middle of	no meio de *noo may-oo djee*
in two days' time	daqui a/dentro de dois dias *da-kee a/den-troo djee doyss djee-ass*
last night	ontem à noite *on-tayn ah noy-tchee*
the day after tomorrow	depois de amanhã *deh-poyss djee a-man-yan*

the day before yesterday	anteontem *an-tchee-on-tayŋ*
today	hoje *oh-Jee*
tomorrow	amanhã *a-man-yaŋ*
tomorrow morning/ afternoon/evening	amanhã de manhã/de tarde/de noite *a-man-yaŋ djee man-yaŋ/djee tar-djee/djee noy-tchee*
yesterday	ontem *on-tayŋ*
yesterday morning/ afternoon/evening	ontem de manhã/de tarde/de noite *on-tayŋ djee man-yaŋ/djee tar-djee/djee noy-tchee*

Expressing yourself

I was born in 1975
nasci em 1975
na-see ayŋ meew noh-vee-sen-tooss ee seh-ten-ta ee seen-koo

I came here a few years ago
estive aqui há alguns anos
eess-tchee-vee a-kee ah al-goonz ah-nooss

I spent a month in Brazil last summer
passei um mês no Brasil no verão passado
pa-say oom mehss no bra-zeew noo veh-rowŋ pass-ah-doo

I was here last year at the same time
estive aqui no ano passado na mesma época
eess-tchee-vee a-kee noo ah-noo pass-ah-doo na meJ-ma eh-poh-ka

what day is it today?	**the 1st of May**
que dia é hoje?	primeiro de maio
keh djee-a eh oh-Jee?	*pree-may-roo djee my-oo*
I'm staying until Sunday	**we're leaving tomorrow**
fico até domingo	a gente vai amanhã
fee-koo a-teh doh-meeŋ-goo	*a Jen-tchee va-ee a-man-yaŋ*

I already have plans for Tuesday
já tenho planos para terça
Jah ten-yoo plah-nooss pah-ra tair-sa

Understanding

de madrugada	in the small hours/early in the morning
todas as segundas	every Monday
todos os dias	every day
três vezes por hora/por dia	three times an hour/a day
uma vez/duas vezes	once/twice

foi construído/construída em meados do século XIX
it was built in the mid-nineteenth century

no verão tem muita gente
it gets very busy here in the summer

você volta quando?
when are you leaving?

quanto tempo você vai ficar?
how long are you staying?

THE TIME

> **Some informal expressions**
>
> **à uma em ponto** at one on the dot
> **pouco depois das oito** just after eight
> **eram dez e pouco** it was just after ten

The basics

half an hour	meia hora *may-a oh-ra*
in the afternoon	de tarde *djee tar-djee*
in the morning	de manhã *djee man-yaη*
midday	meio-dia *may-oo djee-a*
midnight	meia-noite *may-a noy-tchee*
on time	na hora *na oh-ra*
a quarter past ...	... e quinze ... *ee keen-zee*
a quarter to ...	quinze para ... *keen-zee pah-ra ...*
half past...	...e meia ... *ee may-a*

Expressing yourself

what time is it?
que horas são?
keh oh-rass sown?

excuse me, have you got the time, please?
desculpe, você poderia me dizer as horas?
dess-kool-pee, vo-seh poh-deh-ree-a mee dee-zair ass oh-rass?

it's exactly three o'clock
são três horas em ponto
sown trehz oh-rass ayŋ pon-too

it's nearly one o'clock
é quase uma hora
eh kwah-zee oo-ma oh-ra

it's ten past one
é uma e dez
eh oo-ma ee dehss

it's a quarter past one
é uma e quinze
eh oo-ma ee keen-zee

it's a quarter to one
faltam quinze para a uma
fal-towŋ keen-zee pah-ra a oo-ma

it's twenty past twelve
é meio-dia e vinte
eh may-oo djee-a ee veen-tchee

it's twenty to twelve
são vinte para o meio-dia
sown veen-tchee pah-ra oo may-oo djee-a

it's half past one
é uma e meia
eh oo-ma ee may-a

I arrived at about two o'clock
cheguei por volta das duas
sheh-gay poor vol-ta dass doo-ass

I set my alarm for nine
coloquei o despertador para as nove
koh-loh-kay oo djeess-pair-ta-doH pah-ra ass noh-vee

I waited twenty minutes
esperei vinte minutos
eess-peh-ray veen-tchee mee-noo-tooss

the train was fifteen minutes late/arrived on time
o trem chegou quinze minutos atrasado/chegou na hora
oo trayŋ sheh-goh keen-zee mee-noo-tooz a-tra-zah-doo/sheh-goh na oh-ra

I got home an hour ago
cheguei em casa faz uma hora
*sheh-**gay** ayŋ **kah**-za faz **oo**-ma **oh**-ra*

shall we meet in half an hour?
nos encontramos daqui a meia hora?
*nooz en-kon-**trah**-mooss da-**kee** a **may**-a **oh**-ra?*

I'll be back in a quarter of an hour
volto daqui a quinze minutos
***vol**-too da-**kee** a **keen**-zee mee-**noo**-tooss*

there's a three-hour time difference between ... and ...
há uma diferença de três horas entre ... e ...
*ah **oo**-ma djee-feh-**ren**-sa djee trehss **oh**-rass **en**-tree ... ee ...*

---

saídas na hora inteira e na meia hora
departs on the hour and the half-hour

aberto das 10h às 16h
open from 10am to 4pm

todos os dias às 19h
every evening at seven

dura cerca de uma hora e meia
it lasts around an hour and a half

NUMBERS

How to write and say numbers and prices

R$ 1.923,67	mil novecentos e vinte e três reais e sessenta e sete centavos *meew noh-vee-sen-tooz ee veen-tchee ee trehss Hee-ah-eess ee seh-sen-ta ee seh-tchee sen-tah-vooss*
R$ 123	cento e vinte e três reais *sen-too ee veen-tchee ee trehss Hee-ah-eess*
R$ 0,65	sessenta e cinco centavos *seh-sen-ta ee seeη-koo sen-tah-vooss*

0	zero *zeh-roo*	22	vinte e dois/duas *veen-tchee ee doyss/doo-ass*
1	um/uma *oom/oo-ma*	30	trinta *treen-ta*
2	dois/duas *doyss/doo-ass*	35	trinta e cinco *treen-ta ee seeη-koo*
3	três *trehss*	40	quarenta *kwa-ren-ta*
4	quatro *kwah-troo*	50	cinqüenta *seeη-kwen-ta*
5	cinco *seeη-koo*	60	sessenta *seh-sen-ta*
6	seis *sayss*	70	setenta *seh-ten-ta*
7	sete *seh-tchee*	80	oitenta *oy-ten-ta*
8	oito *oy-too*	90	noventa *noh-ven-ta*
9	nove *noh-vee*	100	cem *sayη*
10	dez *dess*	101	cento e um/uma *sen-too ee oom/oo-ma*
11	onze *on-zee*	200	duzentos/duzentas *doo-zen-tooss/doo-zen-tass*
12	doze *doh-zee*	300	trezentos/trezentas *treh-zen-tooss/treh-zen-tass*
13	treze *treh-zee*	400	quatrocentos/quatrocentas *kwa-troo-sen-tooss/kwa-troo-sen-tass*
14	quatorze *kwa-tor-zee*	500	quinhentos/quinhentas *keen-yen-tooss/keen-yen-tass*
15	quinze *keen-zee*		
16	dezesseis *dez-ee-sayss*		
17	dezessete *dez-ee-seh-tchee*		
18	dezoito *dez-oy-too*		
19	dezenove *dez-ee-noh-vee*		
20	vinte *veen-tchee*		
21	vinte e um/uma *veen-tchee ee oom/oo-ma*		

600	seiscentos/seiscentas *sayss-sen-tooss/sayss-sen-tass*	**1,000**	mil *meew*
700	setecentos/setecentas *seh-tchee-sen-tooss/seh-tchee-sen-tass*	**2,000**	dois/duas mil *doyss/doo-ass meew*
800	oitocentos/oitocentas *oy-too-sen-tooss/oy-too-sen-tass*	**10,000**	dez mil *dess meew*
900	novecentos/novecentas *noh-vee-sen-tooss/noh-vee-sen-tass*	**1,000,000**	um milhão *oom meel yown*

first	primeiro/primeira *pree-may-roo/pree-may-ra*
second	segundo/segunda *seh-goon-doo/seh-goon-da*
third	terceiro/terceira *tair-say-roo/tair-say-ra*
fourth	quarto/quarta *kwar-too/kwar-ta*
fifth	quinto/quinta *keen-too/keen-ta*
sixth	sexto/sexta *sess-too/sess-ta*
seventh	sétimo/sétima *seh-tchee-moo/seh-tchee-ma*
eighth	oitavo/oitava *oy-tah-voo/oy-tah-va*
ninth	nono/nona *noh-noo/noh-na*
tenth	décimo/décima *dess-ee-moo/dess-ee-ma*
twentieth	vigésimo/vigésima *vee-Je-zee-moo/vee-Je-zee-ma*

20 plus 3 equals 23
vinte mais três são vinte e três
veen-tchee ma-eess trehss sown veen-tchee ee trehss

20 minus 3 equals 17
vinte menos três são dezessete
veen-tchee meh-nooss trehss sown dez-ee-seh-tchee

20 multiplied by 4 equals 80
vinte vezes quatro são oitenta
veen-tchee veh-zeess kwah-troo sown oy-ten-ta

20 divided by 4 equals 5
vinte dividido por quatro são cinco
veen-tchee djee-vee-djee-doo poor kwah-troo sown seen-koo

NUMBERS

DICTIONARY

ENGLISH-PORTUGUESE

A

a um *m*/uma *f*

able: to be able to ser capaz de

about *(with numbers)* cerca de; *(with time)* por volta de; **to be about to** estar prestes a; **a book about ...** um livro sobre ...

above *(level)* acima; *(number, quantity)* mais de; *(positioned)* por cima de, sobre; **above sea level** acima do nível do mar; **the floor above** o andar de cima

abroad no exterior; **to go abroad** ir para o exterior

accent sotaque *m*

accept aceitar

accident acidente *m* **32, 115**; **to have an accident** sofrer um acidente

accommodation alojamento *m*

ache dor *f*

across do outro lado de; **the hotel across the road** o hotel do outro lado da rua; **to travel across the country** viajar pelo país; **to walk across a bridge/the road** atravessar uma ponte/a rua

adaptor adaptador *m*

address endereço *m*

addressee destinatário*m*/destinatária *f*

admission entrada *f*

adult adulto *m*/a *f*

advance: in advance adiantado *m*/adiantada *f*; **advance booking** reserva *f* antecipada

advice conselho *m*; **to ask someone's advice** pedir um conselho a alguém

advise aconselhar

aeroplane avião *m*

afraid: to be afraid of ter medo de

after *(in time)* depois (de), após; *(in space)* atrás de

afternoon tarde *f*; **good afternoon!** boa tarde!

after-sun (cream) creme *m* hidratante

again outra vez, de novo

against contra

age idade *f*

ago atrás; **a long time ago** faz muito tempo

agree concordar

air ar *m*; **by air** por avião; **in the open air** ao ar livre

air conditioning ar-condicionado *m*

airline companhia *f* aérea

airmail correio *m* aéreo; **by airmail** por avião

airport aeroporto *m*

alarm clock despertador *m*

alcohol álcool *m*

alive vivo *m*/viva *f*

all *(everything)* tudo; *(with singular noun)* todo *m*/toda *f*; *(with plural noun)* todos *mpl*/todas *fpl*; **all inclusive** tudo incluído; **all day** todo o dia; **all week** toda a semana

allergic alérgico *m*/alérgica *f* **111, 112**

almost quase

alone só; **leave me alone!** deixe-me em paz!

already já

also também

although embora, apesar de

always sempre

ambulance ambulância *f* **109**

American americano *m*/americana *f*

among entre

anaesthetic anestesia *f*

and e

angry zangado *m*/zangada *f*

animal animal *m*

ankle tornozelo *m*

annoy irritar

another outro *m*/outra *f*

answer *(n)* resposta *f*

answer *(v)* responder

ant formiga *f*

antibiotic antibiótico *m*

antique antiguidade *f*

anybody, anyone *(in statements)* qualquer um *m*/qualquer uma *f*; *(in questions)* alguém

anything *(in statements)* qualquer coisa; *(in questions)* alguma coisa

anyway de qualquer maneira

appendicitis apendicite *f*

appointment *(with doctor)* consulta f; **to make an appointment** marcar um encontro **109**; **to have an appointment (with)** ter um encontro (com) **109**

April abril m

area área f, região f; **in the area** na região, na área

arm braço m

around *(approximately)* por volta de, cerca de; **around here/there** por aqui/aí; **around midnight** por volta da meia-noite; **I'm just looking around** estou só olhando; **to travel around the country** viajar pelo país

arrange organizar; **to arrange to meet (sb)** organizar um encontro (com alguém)

arrival chegada f

art arte f

article artigo m

artist artista mf

as como; **as soon as possible** logo que possível; **as soon as** assim que, logo que; **as well as** bem como

ashtray cinzeiro m

ask *(enquire)* perguntar; *(request)* pedir; **to ask a question** fazer uma pergunta; **to ask a favour** pedir um favor

aspirin aspirina f

asthma asma f

at em; **at the hotel** no hotel; **at night/2am** à noite/às duas da manhã; **at midnight** à meia-noite

atmosphere ambiente m

at sign arroba f

attack *(n)* ataque m

attack *(v)* atacar **116**

attention atenção f

August agosto m

autumn outono m

available disponível

avenue avenida f

average média f

away: to go away ir embora; **ten kilometres away** a dez quilômetros (daqui)

B

baby bebê mf

baby's bottle mamadeira f

back *(of person)* costas fpl; *(of thing)* parte f de trás

backpack mochila f

bad *(person, weather)* mau m/má f, ruim; *(food)* estragado m/estragada f; **not bad** nada mal

badly mal

bag *(plastic, paper)* saco m; *(handbag)* mala f

baggage bagagem f

baker's, bakery padaria f

balcony varanda f

ball *(for playing)* bola f; *(dance)* baile m

ballet balé m

band banda f

bandage atadura f

bank banco m **94**; **bank account** conta f (bancária)

banknote nota f

bar *(place)* bar m; *(counter)* balcão m

barbecue churrasco m; **barbecue restaurant** churrascaria f

bargain pechincha f

basketball basquete m

bath banho m; *(bathtub)* banheira f; **to have a bath** tomar banho; **bath towel** toalha f de banho

bathrobe roupão m

bathroom banheiro m; **ensuite bathroom** banheiro m privativo

battery *(of radio, watch)* pilha f; *(of car)* bateria f **32**

be *(referring to intrinsic quality, role)* ser; *(referring to changeable state)* estar; *(exist)* ter; **I am a teacher** sou professora; **it's cold** está frio; **we are on holiday** estamos de férias; **is there a restaurant nearby?** tem algum restaurante aqui perto?; **I'm 25 years old** tenho 25 anos; **how are you?** como você está?

beach praia f; **beach towel** toalha f de praia

beard barba f

beautiful lindo m/linda f, belo m/bela f

because porque; **because of** por causa de

bed cama f

before antes (de)

begin começar

beginner principiante mf

beginning início m; **at the beginning** no início

behind atrás (de)

believe acreditar

below *(certain level)* abaixo; *(under)* debaixo; **below zero** abaixo de zero; **the floor below** o andar debaixo

belt cinto *m*
beside ao lado de, junto a
best melhor; **the best** o melhor *m*/a melhor *f*
better melhor; **to get better** melhorar; **it's better to …** é melhor …
between entre
bicycle bicicleta *f*
big grande
bike *(bicycle)* bicicleta *f*; *(motorcycle)* motocicleta *f*
bill conta *f* **41, 52**
bin lixeira *f*
bird pássaro *m*; *(poultry)* ave *f*
birthday aniversário *m*; **happy birthday** feliz aniversário!
bit pedaço *m*
bite *(n) (from animal)* mordida *f*; *(from insect)* picada *f*; *(of food)* dentada *f*
bite *(v) (person, animal)* morder; *(insect)* picar
bitter amargo *m*/amarga *f*
black negro *m*/negra *f*, preto *m*/preta *f*; **black and white** *(film)* em preto-e-branco
blackout desmaio *m*
blanket cobertor *m*
bleed sangrar
blind cego *m*/cega *f*
blister bolha *f*
blood pressure pressão *f* arterial
blood sangue *m*
blue azul
board *(v)* embarcar **25**
boat barco *m*
body corpo *m*
bone osso *m*
book *(n)* livro *m*
book *(v)* reservar **23, 33**
bookshop livraria *f*
boot *(shoe)* bota *f*; *(car)* porta-malas *f*
booth *(phone, photo)* cabine *f*
border fronteira *f*
boring chato *m*/chata *f*
boss chefe *mf*
both ambos *m*/ambas *f*; **both of us** nós dois *m*/nós duas *f*
bottle garrafa *f*; **bottle opener** abridor *m* de garrafas
bottom *(of person)* traseiro *m*; *(of thing)* fundo *m*; **at the bottom (of)** no fundo (de)
bowl tigela *f*
box caixote *m*

boy menino *m*
boyfriend namorado *m*
bra sutiã *m*
bracelet pulseira *f*
brake *(n)* freio *m*
brake *(v)* freiar
Brazil Brasil *m*
Brazilian brasileiro *m*/brasileira *f*
bread pão *m*
break quebrar **109**; **to break one's leg** quebrar a perna; **to break into** arrombar **116**; **to break down** *(car)* pifar **32, 116**
breakdown pane *f*; **breakdown service** pronto-socorro *m*
breakfast café da manhã *m* **40**; **to have breakfast** tomar o café da manhã
bridge ponte *f*
briefcase pasta *f*
bring trazer
Britain Grã-Bretanha *f*
British britânico *m*/britânica *f*
broken quebrado *m*/quebrada *f*
brother irmão *m*
brown castanho *m*/castanha *f*
bruise mancha *f* roxa
brush escova *f*
build construir
building edifício *m*
bump *(n) (on head)* galo *m*; *(on arm, leg)* inchaço *m*
bumper pára-choque *m*
bureau de change casa *f* de câmbio
burn *(n)* queimadura *f*
burn *(v)* queimar; **to burn oneself** queimar-se
burst arrebentar
bus ônibus *m* **28, 29**; **bus station** *(estação)* rodoviária *f*; **bus stop** parada *f* de ônibus
business negócios *mpl*; **on business** a negócios; **business trip** viagem *f* de negócios; **business class** classe *f* executiva
busy *(person)* ocupado *m*/ocupada *f*; *(place, street)* movimentado *m*/movimentada *f*
but mas
butcher's açougue *m*
button botão *m*
buy comprar **23, 84, 86**
by *(place)* em; *(means)* de; *(agent)* por; **by the window** na janela; **by car** de carro
bye! tchau!

C

cable *(of appliance)* fio m; **cable TV** tevê f a cabo
café café m
calf *(of leg)* barriga f da perna
call *(n)* chamada f, ligação f; **to make a call** fazer uma ligação
call *(v)* chamar **105**; **to be called** chamar-se
call back *(phone)* ligar de voltar **105**
calm calmo m/calma f
camcorder câmera f de vídeo
camera máquina f fotográfica, câmera f
camping acampar; **to go camping** fazer camping
campsite camping m **44**
can *(n)* lata f; **can opener** abridor m de latas
can *(v)* *(be able, allowed)* poder; *(know how)* saber; *(have the capacity)* conseguir
cancel cancelar
canoeing canoagem f; **to go canoeing** fazer canoagem
cap boné m
car carro m; **by car** de carro; **car park** estacionamento m
card *(for information, greetings)* cartão m; *(playing card)* carta f
care cuidado m
carefully com cuidado
carriage vagão m
carry levar
case: in case of em/no caso de
cash dinheiro m; **to pay cash** pagar em dinheiro **85**
cashier caixa m
cashpoint caixa m automático **94**
casualty (department) emergência f
cat gato m
catch pegar
cathedral catedral f
Catholic católico m/católica f
celebrate festejar
cell phone celular m
centimetre centímetro m
centre centro m
century século m
chair cadeira f
chance: by chance por acaso
change *(n)* *(alteration)* mudança f; *(money)* troco m **52, 84, 85**; *(currency exchange)* câmbio m
change *(v)* *(money)* trocar **94**; *(clothes, place)* mudar de; *(transport)* fazer transbordo
changing room vestiário m **87**
channel canal m
chapel capela f
charge *(n)* *(price)* preço m
charge *(v)* *(price)* cobrar
cheap barato m/barata f
check verificar
check in *(hotel)* registrar-se; *(airport)* fazer check-in
check-in *(n)* check-in m **25**
check out entregar a chave
check-out *(in shop)* caixa f
chemist's farmácia f
cheque cheque m
chequebook talão m de cheques
chess xadrez m
chest peito m
chewing gum chiclete m
child criança f
chilly frio m/fria f
chin queixo m
chocolate chocolate m
choice escolha f
choose escolher
Christmas Natal; **Happy Christmas!** Feliz Natal!
church igreja f
cigar charuto m
cigarette cigarro m
cinema cinema m
circulation circulação f
city cidade f
class classe f
clean *(adj)* limpo m/limpa f
clean *(v)* limpar
cleaning limpeza f
climate clima m
climbing montanhismo m; **to go climbing** praticar montanhismo
cloakroom guarda-volumes m
clock relógio m
close *(v)* fechar
closed fechado m/fechada f
closing time horário m de fechamento
cloth pano m
clothes roupa f
cloud nuvem f

club clube m; (disco) discoteca f
clutch embreagem f
coach (bus) ônibus m; (part of train) vagão m
coast costa f
coastguard guarda-costeira f
coathanger cabide m
code código m **106**
coffee café m
coin moeda f
cold (adj) frio m/fria f; **it's cold** está fazendo frio; **I'm cold** tenho/estou com frio
cold (n) (low temperature) frio m; (illness) gripe f; **to have a cold** ter gripe
collection coleção f; (mail) coleta f
colour cor f **87**; **colour film** filme m colorido
comb pente m
come vir; **to come back** regressar; **to come in** entrar; **to come out** sair; **I come from London** sou de Londres
comfortable confortável
commerce comércio m
commission comissão f **94**
company companhia f
complain queixar-se, reclamar
comprehensive insurance seguro m completo
computer computador m
concert concerto m
concession desconto m **23, 73**
condom camisinha m, preservativo m
confirm confirmar **26**
connection ligação f **26**
constipated com prisão de ventre
consulate consulado m **115**
contact (n) contato m; **contact lenses** lentes fpl de contato
contact (v) entrar em contato com **104**
contagious contagioso m/contagiosa f
continuation continuação f
continue continuar
contraceptive anticoncepcional m
contract contrato m
cook (v) cozinhar
cooking cozinha f; **to do the cooking** cozinhar
cool fresco m/fresca f
copy (n) cópia f
copy (v) copiar
corkscrew saca-rolhas m
corner (of room) canto m; (of street) esquina f

correct (adj) certo m/certa f, correto m/correta f
correspondence correspondência f
cost (v) custar
cotton algodão m; **cotton bud** cotonete m; **cotton wool** algodão m
cough (n) tosse f; **to have a cough** ter tosse
cough (v) tossir
count contar; **to count on** contar com
counter balcão m
country país m
countryside campo m
course curso m; **of course** é claro
cover (n) (of jar) tampa f; (of book) capa f
cover (v) cobrir
cream creme m
credit card cartão m de crédito **41, 52, 85**
crisis crise f
cross (n) cruz f
cross (v) (street) atravessar
cruise cruzeiro m
cup xícara f
cure curar
currency moeda f
current corrente f
cushion almofadinha f
customs alfândega f; **customs duty** imposto m alfandegário
cut cortar; **to cut oneself** cortar-se
cutlery talher m
cycle path ciclovia f **80**
cycling ciclismo m

D

damaged danificado m/danificada f
damp úmido m/úmida f
dance (n) dança f
dance (v) dançar
dangerous perigoso m/perigosa f
dark escuro m/escura f; **dark blue** azul-escuro
date (n) data f; **date of birth** data f de nascimento
daughter filha f
day dia m; **the day after tomorrow** depois de amanhã; **the day before yesterday** anteontem
dead morto m/morta f
deaf surdo m/surda f
dear querido m/querida f; (expensive) caro

m/cara *f*

debit card cartão *m* de débito

December dezembro

decide decidir

declare declarar

decrease diminuir

deep (pro)fundo *m*/(pro)funda *f*

degree *(level)* grau *m*

delay atraso *m*, demora *f*

delayed atrasado *m*/atrasada *f*

delete apagar

dentist dentista *mf*

deodorant desodorante *m*

depart partir

department store loja *f* de departamentos

departure partida *f*

depend (on) depender (de)

deposit depósito *m*

details dados *mpl*

develop revelar

diabetes diabetes *m*

dial discar

dialling code código *m* de área

diarrhoea: to have diarrhoea ter diarréia

dictionary dicionário *m*

die *(v)* morrer

difference diferença *f*

different (from) diferente (de)

difficult difícil

digital camera máquina digital *f*, câmera digital *f*

dinner jantar *m*; **to have dinner** jantar

direct direto *m*/direta *f*

direction direção *f*

directory lista *f* telefônica; **directory enquiries** informações *fpl*

dirty *(adj)* sujo *m*/suja *f*

disabled deficiente **116**

disappear desaparecer

disappointing decepcionante

disaster desastre *m*

disco discoteca *f*

discount desconto *m* **73**; **to give someone a discount** fazer um desconto a alguém; **discount fare** tarifa *f* reduzida

discover descobrir

discuss discutir

dish prato *m*; **dish of the day** prato do dia

dishes *(crockery)* louça *f*; **to do the dishes** lavar a louça

dishwasher máquina *f* de lavar louça

disinfect desinfetar

disposable razor gilete *m*

disturb incomodar; **do not disturb** não incomodar

dive mergulhar

diving mergulho *m*; **to go diving** mergulhar

do fazer

doctor médico *m*/médica *f* **108, 115**

document documento *m*

dog cachorro *m*

door porta *f*

double: double bed cama *f* de casal; **double room** quarto *m* duplo

down para baixo; **down the street** rua abaixo; **to go down** descer

downstairs andar *m* de baixo; **I live downstairs** moro no andar de baixo; **to go/come downstairs** descer

draught beer chope *m*

dress *(n)* vestido *m*

dress *(v)* vestir; **to get dressed** vestir-se

dressing *(for wound)* curativo *m*

drink *(n)* bebida *f*; *(alcoholic)* drinque *m*; **to go for a drink** ir beber um drinque **47, 65**

drink *(v)* beber

drinking water água *f* potável

drive: *(n)* **to go for a drive** ir dar uma volta de carro

drive *(v)* conduzir

driver motorista *mf*

driving licence carteira *f* de motorista

drops gotas *fpl*

drown afogar-se

drugstore drogaria *f*

dry *(adj)* seco *m*/seca *m*

dry *(v)* secar

dry-cleaner's lavanderia *f* a seco

dual carriageway via *f* rápida

dummy chupeta *f*

duration duração *f*

during durante; **during the week** durante a semana

dustbin lata *f* de lixo

duty dever *m*; **duty chemist** farmácia *f* 24 horas

E

each cada; **each one** cada um

ear *(outer part only)* orelha *f*; *(organ)* ouvido *m*

earache dor *f* de ouvido
early cedo
earn ganhar
earplug tampão *m* para o ouvido
earrings brincos *mpl*
east leste *m*; **in the east** no leste; **(to the) east of** a leste de
Easter Páscoa *f*; **Happy Easter!** Feliz Páscoa!
easy fácil
eat comer **47**
economy class classe *f* econômica
Elastoplast® adesivo *m*
elderly idoso *m*/idosa *f*
electric elétrico *m*/elétrica *m*; **electric shaver** barbeador *m* elétrico
electricity eletricidade *f*
elevator elevador *m*
e-mail e-mail *m*; **e-mail address** (endereço *m* de) e-mail *m* **100**
embassy embaixada *f*
emergency emergência *f* **115**; **in an emergency** em caso de emergência; **emergency exit** saída *f* de emergência
empty vazio *m*/vazia *f*
end fim *m*; **at the end of** no fim de; **at the end of the street** ao fundo da rua
engaged *(phone)* ocupado *m*/ocupada *f*; *(to be married)* noivo *m*/noiva *f*
engine motor *m*
England Inglaterra *f*
English inglês *m*/inglesa *f*; *(language)* inglês *m*
enjoy gostar de; **enjoy your meal!** bom apetite!; **to enjoy oneself** divertir-se
enough suficiente; **that's enough!** já chega!
en-suite com banheiro privativo
enter entrar; *(data)* digitar
entertaining divertido *m*/divertida *f*
entrance entrada *f*
envelope envelope *m*
epileptic epiléptico *m*/epiléptica *f*
equipment equipamento *m*
Europe Europa *f*
European europeu *m*/européia *f*
even if mesmo que
evening noite *f*; **in the evening** à noite
ever: have you ever been to Porto Alegre? já esteve em Porto Alegre?
every todos *mpl*/todas *fpl*; **every day** todos os dias; **every week** todas as semanas
everybody, everyone todo mundo, todos

everywhere por todo o lado
example: for example por exemplo
excellent excelente
except exceto
excess excesso *m*; **excess luggage** excesso de bagagem
exchange rate taxa *f* de câmbio
excursion excursão *f*
excuse *(n)* desculpa *f*
excuse *(v)* desculpar; **excuse me!** desculpe!
exhaust pipe cano *m* de descarga
exhausted exausto *m*/exausta *f*
exhibition exposição *f*
exit saída *f*
expensive caro *m*/cara *f*
expiry date data *f* de vencimento
explain explicar
express: by express post por correio prioritário
extra extra
extraordinary extraordinário *m*/ extraordinária *f*
eye olho *m*

F

fabric tecido *m*
face cara *f*; rosto *m*
fact fato *m*; **in fact** na verdade
faint desmaiar
fair *(n)* feira *f*
fall *(v)* cair; **to fall asleep** adormecer; **to fall ill** adoecer
false falso *m*/falsa *f*
family família *f*; **family name** nome *m* de família
fan ventilador *m*; *(sport)* torcedor *m*/torcedora *f*
far longe; **far from** longe de; **far away** muito longe
fare bilhete *m*
fashion moda *f*
fast rápido *m*/rápida *f*
fat gordo *m*/gorda *f*
father pai *m*
favour favor *m*; **to do someone a favour** fazer um favor a alguém
favourite favorito *m*/favorita *f*
February fevereiro
feel sentir **110**; **to feel good/bad** sentir-se bem/mal; **to feel dizzy** sentir tonturas; **to**

feel sick estar enjoado/enjoada
feeling sentimento *m*
ferry balsa *f*
festival festival *m*
fever febre *f*; **to have a fever** estar com febre
few poucos *mpl*/poucas *fpl*; **a few** alguns *mpl*/ algumas *fpl*; **quite a few** vários *mpl*/várias *fpl*
fiancé noivo *m*
fiancée noiva *f*
file arquivo *m*
fill encher; **to fill in/out** *(form)* preencher
filling *(in tooth)* obturação *f*
film filme *m* **91**
finally por último
find achar, encontrar
fine *(n)* multa *f*
fine *(adj)* bem; **I'm fine** estou bem
finger dedo *m*
finish acabar
fire incêndio *m*; fogo *m*
first primeiro *m*/primeira *f*; **first (of all)** primeiro, antes de mais; **first aid** primeiros-socorros *mpl*; **first class** primeira classe *f*; **first floor** primeiro andar *m*; **first name** nome *m* de batismo, nome *m*
fish *(v)* pescar
fishmonger's peixaria *f*
fitting room cabine *f* de provas
fizzy gaseificado *m*/gaseificada *f*
flat *(n)* apartamento *m*
flat *(adj) (level)* plano *m*/plana *f*; *(rate)* fixo *m*/fixa *f*; *(battery)* descarregada; *(tyre)* vazio
flavour sabor *m*
flaw defeito *m*
flight vôo *m*
flip-flops Havaianas® *fpl*
flippers nadadeiras *fpl*
floor *(n) (of room)* chão *m*; *(storey)* andar *m*; **on the floor** no chão
flower flor *f*
flu gripe *f*
fly *(n)* mosca *f*
fly *(v)* voar
follow seguir
food comida *f*; **food poisoning** intoxicação *f* alimentar
foot pé *m*; **by/on foot** a pé
football futebol *m*; **football match** partida *f* de futebol; **football pitch** campo *m* de futebol
for para; *(time)* durante; **for an hour** durante uma hora
forecast previsão *f*
forehead testa *f*
foreign estrangeiro *m*/estrangeira *f*
foreigner estrangeiro *m*/estrangeira *f*
forest floresta *f*
forget esquecer-se (de)
fork garfo *m*
form ficha *f*, formulário *m*
forward *(adj) (in front)* da frente
forward *(adv)* para a frente; **to move forward** andar para a frente
fracture fratura *f*
fragile frágil
free *(unoccupied, unrestrained)* livre; *(with no charge)* grátis, de graça, gratuito
freezer congelador *m*
Friday sexta-feira *f*
fridge frigorífico *m*
friend amigo *m*/amiga *f*
from de; **from ... to ...** de ... a ...; **from now on** daqui em diante
front frente *f*; **in front of** em/à frente de; **in front of me/us** à minha/nossa frente
frozen congelado *m*/congelada *f*
frying pan frigideira *f*
full cheio *m*/cheia *f*; *(restaurant)* lotado; **full name** nome *m* completo
fully inclusive com tudo incluído
funfair feira *f* popular
funny engraçado *m*/engraçada *f*
furnished mobiliado *m*/mobiliada *f*
fuse fusível *m*

G

game jogo *m*, partida *f*; **to have a game of ...** disputar uma partida de ...
garage *(for repair)* oficina *f* **32**; *(for parking)* garagem *f*
garden jardim *m*
gas gás *m*; **gas cylinder** botijão *m* de gás
gate *(in airport)* portão *m* de embarque; *(in garden)* portão *m*
gay gay, homossexual
gearbox caixa *f* de câmbio
general geral
gents' (toilet) (toalete *m* dos) homens
get *(train, bus, illness)* pegar; *(obtain)* obter;

(receive) receber; (fetch) ir buscar; **to get better** melhorar; **to get by** virar-se; **to get off** (out of bus, car) descer; **to get up** levantar-se; **to get worse** piorar
gift wrap embrulhar para presente
girl menina f
girlfriend (female friend) amiga f; (partner) namorada f
give dar; **to give back** devolver; **to give up** desistir
glass vidro m; (for drinking) copo m; **a glass of water/of wine** um copo de água/de vinho
glasses óculos mpl
gloves luvas fpl
gluten-free sem glúten
go ir; **to go to Pernambuco/to Argentina** ir para Pernambuco/para a Argentina; **to go away** ir embora; **to go in** entrar; **to go out** sair; **to go out with someone** sair com alguém; **to go with** ir com
goggles óculos mpl de proteção
gold ouro m; (adj) de ouro
golf golfe m; **golf course** campo m de golfe
good bom m/boa f; **good morning** bom dia; **good afternoon** boa tarde; **good evening** boa noite
goodbye adeus
goodnight boa noite
GP clínico m geral
grams gramas mpl
grass grama f
great (very good) ótimo m/ótima f, espetacular; **great!** ótimo!
Great Britain Grã-Bretanha f
green verde
greengrocer's verdureiro m
grey cinzento m/cinzenta f
grocer's mercearia f
ground floor (andar) m térreo
group grupo m
grow crescer
guarantee garantia f
guest hóspede mf; **guest house** pousada f
guide (person) guia mf
guidebook guia m
guided tour visita f guiada
gynaecologist ginecologista mf

H

hair (on head) cabelo m; (on body, animal)

pêlo m
hairdresser cabeleireiro m/cabeleireira f
hairdrier secador m de cabelo
half metade f; **half a litre/kilo** meio litro/quilo; **half an hour** meia hora
hand mão f; **hand luggage** bagagem f de mão **25**; **hand towel** toalha f de rosto
handbag mala f
handball handebol m
handbrake freio m de mão
handicapped deficiente
handicraft artesanato m
handkerchief lenço m (de mão)
hand-made feito m/feita f à mão
hang up (telephone) desligar
hangover ressaca f
happen acontecer
hard (not soft) duro/dura; (difficult) difícil
hardly: you can hardly see it mal se vê
hat chapéu m
hate (v) detestar
have ter; **to have to** ter que; **I have to go** tenho que ir
he ele
head cabeça f
headache dor f de cabeça; **to have a headache** ter dor de cabeça
headlight farol (dianteiro) m
heal cicatrizar
health saúde f
hear ouvir
heart coração m; **heart attack** ataque m cardíaco
heat (n) calor m
heater aquecedor m; **electric/gas heater** aquecedor elétrico/a gás
heating aquecimento m
heavy (suitcase, food) pesado m/pesada f; (rain, traffic) intenso m/intensa f
heel salto m
hello olá; (on phone) alô
helmet capacete m
help (n) ajuda f; **to call for help** pedir socorro; **help!** socorro!, ajuda!
help (v) ajudar **115**
her (adj) dela; **her luggage** a bagagem dela; **her friends** os amigos dela
her (pron) (direct object) a; (indirect object) lhe; (after preposition) ela; **I know her** eu a conheço; **I asked her** eu perguntei a ela;

for her para ela
here aqui; **here is/are** aqui está/estão
hers dela; **a friend of hers** um amigo dela; **they are hers** são dela; **hers are here** os/as dela estão aqui
herself *(reflexive)* se; *(after preposition)* ela (própria); **she hurt herself** ela se machucou
hi oi
high alto m/alta f; **high blood pressure** pressão f alta
hill monte m
him *(direct object)* o; *(indirect object)* lhe; *(after preposition)* ele; **I know him** eu o conheço; **I asked him** eu perguntei a ele; **for him** para ele; **it's him** é ele
himself *(reflexive)* se; *(after preposition)* ele (próprio); **he hurt himself** ele se machucou
hip quadril m
hire *(n)* aluguel m
hire *(v) (car, bike)* alugar **33, 77, 80**
his dele; **his luggage** a bagagem dele; **his friends** os amigos dele; **a friend of his** um amigo dele; **they are his** são dele; **his are here** os/as dele estão aqui
history história f
hitchhike pedir carona
hockey hóquei m
hold *(retain, contain)* segurar; *(party)* organizar; *(on phone)* esperar; **hold on!** *(on the phone)* não desligue!
hole buraco m
holiday(s) férias fpl; **on holiday** de férias
home casa f; **at home** em casa; **to go home** voltar para casa
homemade caseiro m/caseira f
homosexual homossexual
honeymoon lua-de-mel f
hope esperar
horse cavalo m
horseriding equitação f
hospital hospital m
hot quente; **the soup is hot** a sopa está quente; **it's hot** *(weather)* está calor
hotel hotel m **40**
hour hora f; **an hour and a half** uma hora e meia
house casa f
how como; **how are you?** como está?; **how are things?** tudo bom?; **how much**
quanto; **how much is it?** quanto custa?; **(for) how long?** há quanto tempo?
humid úmido m/úmida f
hunger fome f
hungry: to be hungry ter fome
hurry pressa; **to be in a hurry** estar com pressa
hurry (up) apressar-se; **hurry up!** depressa!
hurt doer; **it hurts** dói **110**; **my head hurts** me dói a cabeça
husband marido m
hypermarket hipermercado m

I

I eu; **I'm English** sou inglês/inglesa; **I'm 22 (years old)** tenho 22 anos
ice gelo m; **ice cube** cubo m de gelo
ID documento m de identificação
idea idéia f
if se
ill doente; **to fall ill** ficar doente
illness doença f
importance importância f
important importante
impressive impressionante
in em; **in 2008/Portuguese** em 2008/português; **in England** na Inglaterra; **in the 19th century** no século dezenove
included incluído m/incluída f **40, 52**
incredible incrível
indicator indicador m
infection infecção f
information informação f **71**
injection injeção f
injured ferido m/ferida f
insect inseto m
insecticide inseticida m
insert inserir
inside *(interior)* interior; **what's inside?** o que tem dentro?; **they're inside** estão lá dentro
instead: instead of em vez de
insurance seguro m
intend to pretender
interesting interessante
international money order transferência f bancária internacional
Internet café cibercafé m **100**
interval intervalo m
invite convidar
invoice fatura f

Irish irlandês *m*/irlandesa *f*
Ireland Irlanda *f*
island ilha *f*
it isso; **it's beautiful** isso é bonito
itch coçar
item *(of clothing)* peça *f*; *(product)* artigo *m*

J

jacket casaco *m*
January janeiro *m*
jar pote *m*
jeans calças *fpl* de brim
jeweller's joalheria *f*
jewellery jóias *fpl*
job emprego *m*
journey viagem *f*
jug jarra *f*
juice suco *m*
July julho *m*
junction cruzamento *m*
June junho *m*
just *(only)* apenas, só; **just a little** só um
    pouquinho; **just before** um pouco antes;
    just one apenas um

K

keep guardar; *(change)* ficar com; *(stay)*
    manter-se
key chave *f* **32, 40, 43**; *(of keyboard)* tecla *f*
keyboard teclado *m*
kidney rim *m*
kill matar
kilo quilo *m*
kilometre quilômetro *m*
kind *(n)* tipo *m*; **what kind of ...?** que tipo
    de ...?
kitchen cozinha *f*
knee joelho *m*
knife faca *f*
know *(person)* conhecer, *(fact)* saber; **I don't
    know** não sei

L

ladies' (toilet) (toalete *m* das) Senhoras
lamp lâmpada *f*
landscape paisagem *f*
language linguagem *f*, língua *f*
last *(adj)* último *m*/última *f*; **last year/month**

no ano/mês passado; **at last** por fim
last *(v)* durar
late atrasado *m*/atrasada *f*, tarde; **to arrive
    late** chegar tarde
launderette lavandaria *f*
lavatory lavatório *m*
lawyer advogado *m*/advogada *f*
leaflet folheto *m*
leak *(n)* *(petrol, gás)* fuga *f*; *(in roof)* goteira *f*
learn aprender
least: the least ... o/a menos ...; **at least**
    pelo menos
leather couro *m*
leave *(depart)* partir; *(behind, alone)* deixar;
    leave me alone! deixe-me em paz!
left esquerdo *m*/esquerda *f*; **to the left (of)**
    à esquerda (de)
left-luggage (office) depósito *m* de bagagem
leg perna *f*
lend emprestar
lens lente *f*
less menos; **less than** menos de
let *(allow)* deixar; *(rent out)* alugar; **let's go!**
    vamos!
letter carta *f*
letterbox caixa *f* do correio
level crossing passagem *f* de nível
lid tampa *f*
lie mentir
lie down deitar-se
life vida *f*
lift elevador *m*
light *(adj)* *(weight, rain, meal)* leve; *(eyes, hair,
    colour)* claro *m*/clara *f*; **light blue** azul-claro
light *(n)* luz *f*; **do you have a light?** tem
    fogo?
light *(v)* acender
light bulb lâmpada *f*
lighter isqueiro *m*
like *(adv)* como; **like this** assim
like *(v)* gostar (de) **18**; **I'd like ...** eu gostaria
    de ...; **I don't like it** não gosto; **I like it a
    lot** gosto muito
line linha *f* **29**
lip lábio *m*
liquid líquido *m*
list lista *f*
listen ouvir
litre litro *m*
little *(adj)* *(time, quantity)* pouco *m*/pouca

f; (size, age) pequeno *m*/pequena *f*; **little time** pouco tempo
little *(adv)* pouco
live *(v)* viver
liver fígado *m*
living room sala *f* de estar
local time hora *f* local
lock *(n) (of door)* fechadura *f*; *(of necklace, suitcase)* fecho *m*
lock *(v)* fechar com chave
long longo *m*/longa *f*; *(hair)* comprido *m*/comprida *f*; **a long time** muito tempo; **how long ... ?** quanto tempo ...?
look *(v)* olhar **87**; *(seem)* parecer; **to look tired** ter ar de cansado *m*/cansada *f*; **look out!** atenção!; **to look after** cuidar de; **to look at** olhar para; **to look for** procurar **84**; **to look like** parecer-se com
lorry caminhão *m*
lose perder **32, 109**; **to get lost** perder-se; **to be lost** estar perdido *m*/perdida *f* **11**
loss perda *f* **94**
lost perdido *m*/perdida *f*
lot: a lot (of) *(singular)* muito *m*/muita *f* (de); *(plural)* muitos *mpl*/muitas *fpl* (de)
loud *(noise, voice)* alto *m*/alta *f*
love *(v)* adorar
low baixo *m*/baixa *f*
luggage bagagem *f* **25, 26**
lunch almoço *m*; **to have lunch** almoçar
lung pulmão *m*
luxury *(adj)* de luxo

M

machine máquina *f*
mad doido *m*/doida *f*
magazine revista *f*
maiden name nome *m* de solteira
mail correio *m*
main principal
make fazer; **to make a mistake** enganar-se; **to make an appointment** marcar um encontro
man homem *m*
manage *(business)* gerenciar; *(cope)* conseguir; *(suitcase, weight)* poder com
manager gerente *mf*
many muitos *mpl*/muitas *fpl*; **how many?** quantos?; **how many times ...?** quantas vezes ...?

map mapa *m* **11, 28, 66**
March março *m*
market mercado *m*
married casado *m*/casada *f*
marvellous: to be marvellous ser uma maravilha
Mass missa *f*
match *(for fire)* fósforo *m*; *(game)* partida *f*
material material *m*
matter: it doesn't matter não importa
mattress colchão *m*
maximum máximo *m*/maxima *f*
May maio *m*
maybe talvez
me me; *(after preposition)* mim; **don't tell me** não me diga; **he knows me** ele me conhece; **it's for me** é para mim; **me too** eu também; **he's with me** ele está comigo; **it's me** sou eu
meal refeição *f*
mean significar; **what does ... mean?** o que significa ... ?
medication, medicine remédio *m*
medium médio *m*/média *f*
meet *(encounter)* encontrar **65, 66**; *(gather)* encontrar-se, reunir-se; **nice to meet you!** muito prazer!
meeting reunião *f*
member membro *m*, sócio *m*
menu cardápio *m* **47**
message mensagem *f*, recado *m* **104**
meter contador *m*
metre metro *m*
microwave microondas *m*
midday meio-dia *m*
middle meio *m*; **in the middle (of)** no meio (de); *(time)* em meados de
midnight meia-noite *f*
mind *(v)* importar-se; **I don't mind** não me importa; **if you don't mind** se você não se importa
mine o(s) meu(s)/a(s) minha(s); **a friend of mine** um amigo meu; **these are mine** estes são meus; **mine are here** os meus/as minhas estão aqui
minimum mínimo *m*/mínima *f*
minute minuto *m*; **at the last minute** na última hora
mirror espelho *m*
miss *(flight, train)* perder **26, 29**; *(be absent)*

faltar **26, 116**; *(long for)* sentir/ter saudades de; **we missed the bus** perdemos o ônibus; **there are two people missing** faltam duas pessoas

Miss Sra.

mistake erro *m* **41, 84**; **to make a mistake** enganar-se

misunderstanding mal-entendido *m*

mobile (phone) celular *m* **103**

modern moderno *m*/moderna *f*

moisturizer creme *m* hidratante

moment momento *m*; **at the moment** neste momento

Monday segunda-feira *f*

money dinheiro *m* **84, 94**

month mês *m*

monument monumento *m*

more mais; **more than** mais de; **much more, a lot more** muito mais; **one more ...** mais um/uma ...

morning manhã *f*

mosquito mosquito *m*

most: the most o/a mais; **most people** a maioria das pessoas

mother mãe *f*

motorbike motocicleta *f*

motorway auto-estrada *f*

mountain montanha *f*

mouth boca *f*

move *(v)* mover; *(oneself)* mover-se

movie filme *m*

Mr Sr.

Mrs Sra.

much: how much? quanto?; **how much is it?, how much does it cost?** quanto custa?

muscle músculo *m*

museum museu *m*

music música *f*

must *(obligation)* ter que; *(certainty)* dever; **it must be 5 o'clock** deve ser cinco horas; **I must go** tenho que ir

my o(s) meu(s)/a(s) minhas; **that's my seat** esse é o meu lugar

myself *(reflexive)* me; *(after preposition)* mim *(próprio m/própria f)*; **I hurt myself** me machuquei

---

N

nail unha *f*; **nail clippers** cortador *m* de unha

name nome *m*; **my name is ...** meu nome é

...; **in the name of** em nome de

nap soneca *f*; **to have a nap** tirar uma soneca

napkin guardanapo *m*

nappy fralda *f*

national holiday feriado *m* nacional

nationality nacionalidade *f*

nature natureza *f*

near perto; **near the beach** perto da praia; **the nearest ...** o/a ... mais perto

necessary necessário *m*/necessária *f*

neck pescoço *m*

necklace colar *m*

need *(v)* precisar de

needle agulha *f*

negative *(film)* negativo *m*

neighbour vizinho *m*/vizinha *f*

neighbourhood bairro *m*

neither nem; **neither ... nor ...** nem ... nem ...; **me neither** eu também não

nervous nervoso *m*/nervosa *f*

never nunca; **never again** nunca mais

new novo *m*/nova *f*; **New Year** Ano *m* Novo

news notícias *fpl*

newspaper jornal *m*

newsstand banca *f* de jornais

next próximo *m*/próxima *f*; **next to ...** junto a ..., próximo de ...; **I go next** sou o próximo

nice *(pleasant)* agradável; *(pretty)* bonito *m*/bonita *f*; *(kind)* simpático *m*/simpática *f*

night noite *f* **39, 42, 44**; **good night!** boa noite!; **at night** à noite

nightclub clube noturno *m*

no não; **no, thank you** não, obrigado *m*/obrigada *f*; **no idea** não tenho idéia

nobody ninguém

noise barulho *m*; **to make a noise** fazer barulho

noisy barulhento *m*/barulhenta *f*

non-alcoholic sem álcool

non-drinking water água *f* não potável

none nenhum *m*/nenhuma *f*

non-smoker não fumante *mf*

noon meio-dia *m*

normal normal

north norte *m*; **in the north** no norte; **(to the) north of** a norte de

nose nariz *m*

not não; **not yet** ainda não; **not at all** *(reply to thanks)* de nada

note nota *m*
notebook caderno *m*
nothing nada
notice aviso *m*
November novembro *m*
now agora; **up to now** até aqui
nowadays hoje em dia
nowhere em lugar nenhum
number número *m*
nurse enfermeiro *m*/enfermeira *f*

O

obvious óbvio *m*/óbvia *f*
occasion ocasião *f*
occupy ocupar
ocean oceano *m*
o'clock: one o'clock uma hora; **three o'clock** três horas
October outubro *m*
of de
offer (*v*) oferecer
often muitas vezes
oil óleo *m*
ointment pomada *f*
OK ok
old velho *m*/velha *f*; **how old are you?** quantos anos você tem?; **old people** os mais velhos
on (*adj*) (*TV, light*) ligado *m*/ligada *f*
on (*prep*) (*position, location*) em; (*about*) sobre; **it's on at …** começa às …; **on Sunday** no domingo; **on holiday** de férias; **on foot** a pé; **on TV/the radio** na televisão/no rádio
once uma vez; **once a day/an hour** uma vez por dia/por hora
one um *m*/uma *f*
online: to go online conectar-se
only apenas, só; **only one** só um
open (*adj*) aberto *m*/aberta *f*
open (*v*) abrir
opening hours horário *m* de funcionamento
opera ópera *f*
operation: to have an operation ser operado *m*/operada *f*
opinion opinião *f*; **in my opinion** na minha opinião
opportunity oportunidade *f*
opposite (*adj*) contrário *m*/contrária *f*; **in the opposite direction** no sentido contrário
opposite (*prep*) em frente a

optician oculista *mf*
or ou
orange (*colour*) cor-de-laranja
orchestra orquestra *f*
order (*n*) (*in restaurant*) encomenda *f*; **out of order** (*phone*) quebrado
order (*v*) (*in restaurant*) fazer o pedido **49, 50**
organic orgânico *m*/orgânica *f*
organize organizar
other outro *m*/outra *f*; **the others** os outros/as outras
otherwise (*or else*) senão; (*differently*) de outro modo
our o(s) nosso(s)/a(s) nossas; **those are our seats** esses são os nossos lugares
ours nosso(s)/nossa(s); **a friend of ours** um amigo nosso; **they are ours** são nossos/nossas; **ours are here** os nossos/as nossas estão aqui
ourselves (*reflexive*) nos; (*after preposition*) nós (próprios *mpl*/próprias *fpl*)
out fora; **get out!** fora!; **to eat out** jantar/almoçar fora; **out of order/service** fora de serviço
outside (*exterior*) exterior *m*; **can we sit outside?** podemos nos sentar lá fora?
outward journey ida *f*
oven forno *m*
over por cima de; **over there** ali
overdone muito passado *m*/passada *f*
overtake ultrapassar
owe dever **52, 85, 111**
own (*adj*) próprio *m*/própria *f*; **my own car** o meu próprio carro
owner proprietário *m*/proprietária *f*; (*of house, restaurant*) dono *m*/dona *m*

P

pack (*v*) (*suitcase*) fazer a mala
packed (*full of people*) lotado *m*/lotada *f*
packet pacote *m*
page página *f*
pain dor *f*
painkiller analgésico *m*
painting quadro *m*, pintura *f*
pair par *m*; **a pair of shoes** um par de sapatos; **a pair of pyjamas** um pijama; **a pair of shorts** um calção
palace palácio *m*
pale pálido *m*/pálida *f*

pants cuecas *fpl*
paper papel *m*; **paper napkin** guardanapo *m* de papel; **paper tissue** lenço *m* de papel
parasol guarda-sol *m*
parcel embrulho *m*; *(post)* encomenda *f*
pardon? como?
parents pais *mpl*
park *(n)* parque *m*
park *(v)* estacionar **31**
parking estacionamento *m*
part parte *f*; **to be a part of** fazer parte de
party festa *f*
pass *(n)* passe *m*
pass *(v)* passar
passenger passageiro *m*/passageira *f*
passport passaporte *m*
password senha *f*
past *(further than)* depois de; **a quarter past ten** dez e quinze
past *(n)* passado *m*
paste *(v) (text)* colar
path caminho *m*
patient *(n)* doente *mf*
pay *(v)* pagar **41, 85, 101**
peace paz *f*
peaceful tranqüilo *m*/tranqüila *f*
pedestrian crossing faixa *f* de segurança
pee fazer xixi
peel *(v)* descascar
pen caneta *f*
pencil lápis *m*
people gente *f*; **a lot of people** muita gente
percent por cento
perfect perfeito *m*/perfeita *f*
perfume perfume *m*
perhaps talvez
person pessoa *f*
personal stereo Walkman® *m*
petrol gasolina *f* **32**; **petrol station** posto *m* de gasolina
phone *(n)* telefone *m*; **phone book** lista *f* telefônica; **phone booth** orelhão *m*; **phone call** telefonema *m*; **to make a phone call** dar um telefonema ; **phone number** número *m* de telefone
phone *(v)* telefonar
phonecard cartão *m* telefônico **103**
photo fotografia *f*; **to take a photo (of)** tirar uma fotografia (de)
photocopy xerox *m*; fotocópia *f*

pick up pegar
pickpocket batedor *m* de carteira
picnic piquenique *m*; **to have a picnic** fazer um piquenique
picturesque pitoresco *m*/pitoresca *f*
piece *(bit)* pedaço *m*; *(of device, machine)* peça *f*; **a piece of** um pedaço de
pill pílula *f*; **to be on the pill** tomar a pílula **111**
pillow almofada *f*
PIN (number) código *m* pessoal, senha *f*
pity: it's a pity é uma pena
place lugar *m*
plan *(n)* plano *m* **65**
plane avião *m*
plant planta *f*
plastic *(n)* plástico *m*; **plastic bag** saco *m* de plástico
plate prato *m*
platform plataforma *f* **29**
play peça *f* de teatro
play *(v) (sport, game)* jogar; *(instrument)* tocar; *(children)* brincar
pleasant agradável
please por favor
pleased satisfeito *m*/satisfeita *f*; **pleased to meet you!** muito prazer!
plug *(on appliance)* tomada *f*; *(for bath, sink)* tampa *f*
plug in ligar
plumber bombeiro *m*
pocket bolso *m*
point *(n)* ponto *m*
point at apontar para
poisonous venenoso *m*/venenosa *f*
police polícia *f*; **police station** delegacia *f* (de polícia) **115**
policeman policial *m*, guarda *m*
policewoman policial *f*
polite educado *m*/educada *f*
poor pobre
port porto *m*
portable portátil
portrait retrato *m*
Portuguese português *m*/portuguesa *f*; *(language)* português *m*
possible possível
post *(n)* correio *m*; **by post** pelo correio; **post office** correio *m* **97**
post *(v)* mandar pelo correio

postage porte *m*
postbox caixa *f* do correio **97**
postcard postal *m*
postcode código *m* postal, CEP *m*
postman carteiro *m*
pot *(for cooking)* panela *f*; *(for tea, coffee)* bule *m*; *(jar)* frasco *m*; **a pot of tea** um bule de chá
powder pó *m*
practical prático *m*/prática *f*
practise praticar
pram carrinho *m* de bebê
prefer preferir
pregnant grávida *f* **110**
prepare preparar
prescription receita *f*
present *(n)* presente *m* **89**
present *(v)* apresentar
press *(v)* apertar
pressure pressão *f*
pretty bonito *m*/bonita *f*
prevent evitar
previous anterior
price preço *m*
priest padre *m*
primary school escola *f* primária
print *(v)* imprimir
probably provavelmente
problem problema *m*
profession profissão *f*
programme programa *m*
promise *(v)* prometer
pronounce pronunciar
propose propor
protect proteger
provide fornecer
public *(adj)* público *m*/pública *f*; **public school** escola *f* privada; **public holiday** feriado *m*; **public transport** transporte *m* público
pull puxar
puncture: I've got a puncture furou o pneu
purple roxo *m*/roxa *f*
purse carteira *f*
push empurrar
pushchair carrinho *m* de bebê
put pôr; **to put something in the bin** colocar algo no lixo; **to put out** *(light, fire)* apagar; **to put up** *(tent)* montar; *(provide accommodation)* alojar; **to put up with**

agüentar
pyjamas pijama *m*

Q

quality qualidade *f*; **of good/poor quality** de boa/má qualidade
quarter quarto *m*; **a quarter of an hour** quinze minutos; **a quarter to ten** quinze para as dez
quay cais *m* (de embarque)
question *(n)* pergunta *f*
queue *(n)* fila *f*
queue *(v)* fazer fila
quick rápido *m*/rápida *f*
quickly rapidamente
quiet *(silent)* silencioso *m*/silenciosa *f*; *(peaceful)* tranqüilo *m*/tranqüila *f*
quite bastante; **quite a lot of money** bastante dinheiro; **quite a lot of things** muitas coisas

R

racist racista *mf*
racket *(tennis, badminton)* raquete *f*
radio rádio *m*; **radio station** estação *f* de rádio
rain *(n)* chuva *f*
rain *(v)* chover; **it's raining** está chovendo
ranch fazenda *f*
rape *(n)* estupro *m*
rape *(v)* estuprar
rare *(infrequent)* raro *m*/rara *f*; *(meat)* mal passado *m*/mal passada *f*
rash irritação *f* na pele
rather *(quite)* bastante; **I'd rather have some juice** prefiro um suco
raw cru *m*/crua *f*
razor gilete *f*; *(electric)* barbeador *m*; **razor blade** lâmina *f* de barbear
reach *(get to)* chegar a
read ler
ready pronto *m*/pronta *f*
reality realidade *f*
reasonable razoável
receipt recibo *m* **85, 111**; *(from cash machine)* comprovante *m*
receive receber
recently recentemente
reception recepção *f*

receptionist recepcionista *mf*
recharge recarregar 103
recipe receita *f*
recognize reconhecer
recommend recomendar 40, 47, 49
record gravar
red *(in colour)* vermelho *m*/vermelha *f*; *(hair)* ruivo *m*/ruiva *f*; **red light** luz *f* vermelha
reduce reduzir
reduction redução *f*
referee árbitro *m*; juíz *m*
refrigerator frigorífico *m*
refund *(n)* reembolso *m*; **to get a refund** ser reembolsado *m*/reembolsada *f* 88
refund *(v)* reembolsar
refuse recusar
region região *f*
registered registado *m*/registada *f*
registration number *(car)* placa *f* do carro
regret lamentar
religion religião *f*
remain ficar
remember lembrar-se (de)
remind recordar
remove remover
rent *(n)* aluguel *m*
rent *(v)* alugar 43
repair *(n)* conserto *m*; **to get something repaired** mandar consertar algo
repair *(v)* consertar 32
repeat repetir 9
report *(v)* dar parte de 26, 94, 117
reserve reservar 48
reserved reservado *m*/reservada *f*
rest *(v)* descansar
rest: *(n)* **the rest** o resto
restaurant restaurante *m*
retired aposentado *m*/aposentada *f*
return *(n)* volta *f*; **return ticket** bilhete *m* de ida e volta
return *(v)* voltar
reverse gear marcha *f* a ré
reverse-charge call ligação *f* a cobrar 103
rheumatism reumatismo *m*
rib costela *f*
rich rico *m*/rica *f*
ride montar
right *(adj)* direito *m*/direita *f*
right *(adv)* **right away** imediatamente; **right beside** mesmo ao lado de

right *(n)* direito *m*; **to have the right to ...** ter o direito de ...; **to the right (of)** à direita (de)
ring *(n)* anel *m*
ringtone sinal *m* de linha
ripe *(adj)* maduro *m*/madura *f*
risk *(n)* risco *m*
river rio *m*
road estrada *f*, via *f*
road sign sinal *m* de trânsito
robbery assalto *m*
rock rocha *f*
roll *(bread)* pão *m*
room quarto *m* 39
round *(adj)* redondo *m*/redonda *f*
roundabout rotatória *f*
route percurso *m*
rubbish lixo *m*; **rubbish bag** saco *m* de lixo
rucksack mochila *f*
run *(v)* correr; *(of bus, train)* circular; *(of machine, car)* funcionar

S

sad triste
safe *(adj)* seguro *m*/segura *f*; **safe deposit box** cofre *m*
safety segurança *f*; **safety belt** cinto *m* de segurança
sailing vela *f*; **to go sailing** velejar
saint santo *m*/santa *f*
sales liquidação *f*
salt sal *m*
salty salgado *m*/salgada *f*
same igual; **(I'll have) the same** (quero) o mesmo/a mesma
sand areia *f*
sandals sandálias *fpl*
sanitary towel absorvente *m* higiênico
satellite TV televisão *f* por satélite
Saturday sábado *m*
saucepan panela *f*
save *(rescue, computer file)* salvar; *(money)* economizar
say dizer; **how do you say ... ?** como se diz ...?; **he said that ...** ele disse que ...
scenery paisagem *f*
school escola *f*
scissors tesoura *f*
Scotland Escócia *f*
Scottish escocês *m*/escocesa *f*

scuba diving mergulho *m*; **to go scuba diving** fazer mergulho
sculpture escultura *f*
sea mar *m*
seafood frutos *mpl* do mar
seashell concha *f*
seasick: to be seasick sentir-se enjoado *m*/enjoada *f*
season (*n*) estação *f* do ano
seat lugar *m* **24**; (*of car, bike*) assento *m*
seatbelt cinto *m* de segurança
second segundo *m*/segunda *f*; **second (of all)** segundo; **second class** segunda classe *f*
secondary school escola *f* secundária
second-hand em segunda mão
section seção *f*
security segurança *f*
see ver; **see you later!** até logo!; **see you soon!** até mais!; **see you tomorrow!** até amanhã!
seem parecer
seldom raramente
select selecionar
self-catering com cozinha
sell vender
Sellotape® Durex® *f*
send enviar
sender remetente *mf*
sense (*n*) sentido *m*
sensible sensato *m*/sensata *f*
sensitive sensível
separate (*adj*) separado *m*/separada *f*
separately separadamente
September setembro *m*
serious (*person*) sério *m*/séria *f*; (*accident, illness*) grave
serve atender
service serviço *m* **52**
several vários *mpl*/várias *fpl*
sex sexo *m*
shade sombra *f*; **in the shade** na sombra
shame vergonha *f*
shampoo xampu *m*
shape forma *f*
share compartilhar
shave (*head, legs*) rapar; (*beard*) fazer a barba
shaving foam espuma de barbear *f*
shawl xale *m*
she ela
sheet (*for bed*) lençol *m*

shirt camisa *f*
shock choque *m*
shoes sapatos *mpl*
shop (*n*) loja *f*; **shop assistant** vendedor *m*/vendedora *f*; **shop window** vitrine *f*
shopkeeper comerciante *mf*
shopping compras *fpl*; **to go shopping** fazer compras
short (*hair, clothes*) curto *m*/curta *f*; (*person*) baixo *m*/baixa *f*; **I'm twenty reais short** estão faltando vinte reais
shorts calções *mpl*
short-sleeved de manga curta
shoulder ombro *m*
show (*n*) espetáculo *m*
show (*v*) mostrar; (*movie*) passar
shower chuveiro *m*, ducha *m*; **to take a shower** tomar uma ducha; **shower gel** gel *m* de banho
shut fechar
shuttle bus navete *f*
shy tímido *m*/tímida *f*
sick doente; **to feel sick** sentir-se enjoado *m*/enjoada *f*
side (*n*) lado *m*
sign (*n*) sinal *m*; (*on road*) placa *f*
sign (*v*) assinar
signal sinal *m*
signature assinatura *f*
silence silêncio *m*
silent silencioso *m*/silenciosa *f*
silk seda *f*
silver prata *f*
silver-plated prateado *m*/prateada *f*
simple simples
since desde
single (*person*) solteiro *m*/solteira *f*; **single (ticket)** passagem *m* só de ida; **single bed** cama *f* de solteiro;
single room quarto *m* individual
sister irmã *f*
sit down sentar-se
size tamanho *m* **88**
skin pele *f*
skirt saia *f*
sky céu *m*
sleep (*n*) sono *m*
sleep (*v*) dormir
sleeping: sleeping bag saco *m* de dormir; **sleeping pill** comprimido *m* para dormir

sleepy: to be sleepy ter sono

sleeve manga f

slice fatia f

slim magro m/magra f

slow lento m/lenta f

slowly lentamente

small pequeno m/pequena f; **small change** dinheiro m trocado

smell (n) cheiro m

smell (v) cheirar; **to smell good/bad** cheirar bem/mal

smoke fumar

smoker fumante mf

smoothie vitamina f

snack lanche m

snorkel tubo m de respiração

so (then) então;(very) tão; **so expensive** tão caro; **so much** tanto; **so many** tantos/tantas; **so that** de forma que

soap sabonete m

soccer futebol m

society sociedade f

socks meia m

sold out esgotado m/esgotada f

some algum m/alguma f; **some people** algumas pessoas

somebody, someone alguém

something alguma coisa; **something else** outra coisa

sometimes às vezes, por vezes

somewhere em algum lugar; **somewhere else** em outro lugar

son filho m

song canção f

soon (in a short time) em breve; (early) cedo; **as soon as** assim que; **it's too soon** é muito cedo; **as soon as possible** o quanto antes; **see you soon** até mais

sore: I have a sore ... dói o meu .../a minha ...

sorry! desculpe!

sound som m

south sul m; **in the south** no sul; **(to the) south of** ao sul de

souvenir recordação f

Spanish (language) espanhol m

spare: spare part peça f sobressalente; **spare tyre** estepe m; **spare wheel** roda f sobressalente

spark plug vela f

sparkling com gás

speak falar **7, 8, 104, 115**

special especial; **today's special** prato m do dia; **special offer** promoção f

speciality especialidade f

speed velocidade f; **at full speed** a toda a velocidade

spell soletrar; **how do you spell it?** como se escreve?

spend (money) gastar; (time, holiday) passar

spicy temperado m/temperada f

spider aranha f

spill derramar

split up separar-se

spoil estragar

sponge esponja f

spoon colher f

sport esporte m

spot (place) local f; (on skin) espinha f

sprain: to sprain one's ankle torcer o pé

spring primavera f

square (adj) quadrado m/quadrada f

square (n) (place) praça f; (shape) quadrado m

stadium estádio m

stain mancha f

stairs escadas fpl

stamp (n) selo m **97**

stand: I can't stand it não suporto isso

start (v) começar

state estado m

statement declaração f

station estação f **29**

statue estátua f

stay (n) estadia f; **enjoy your stay!** boa estadia!

stay (v) ficar; **to be staying at ...** estar hospedado/hospedada em ...; **to stay in touch** manter-se em contato

steal roubar **115**

steering wheel volante m

step (n) degrau m

sticking plaster Band-Aid® m

still (adj) (motionless) imóvel; (not fizzy) sem gás

still (adv) ainda; **one is still missing** ainda falta um

sting (n) picada f

sting (v) picar; **to get stung (by)** ser picado m/picada f (por)

stomach estômago m

stone *(rock)* pedra *f*; *(in fruit)* caroço *m*
stool banco *m*
stop *(n) (bus)* parada *f* **29**
stop *(v)* parar; **without stopping** sem parar
store armazém *m*
storey andar *m*
storm temporal *m*
stove fogão *m*
straight ahead, straight on reto em frente
strange estranho *m*/estranha *f*
street rua *f*; **street market** feira *f*
stroll: to go for a stroll ir passear
strong forte
student estudante *mf* **23**, **73**; **student card**
carteira *f* de estudante
study *(v)* estudar; **to study biology** estudar
biologia
style estilo *m*
subtitled legendado *m*/legendada *f*
subway passagem *f* subterrânea
success êxito *m*
suffer sofrer
suggest sugerir
suit *(n)* terno *m*
suit: it suits you fica bem em você
suitcase mala *f*
summer verão *m*
sun sol *m*; **in the sun** ao sol; **sun cream**
protetor *m* solar
sunbathe tomar banhos de sol
sunburn queimadura *f* do sol
Sunday domingo *m*
sunglasses óculos *mpl* de sol
sunny: it's sunny tem sol
sunrise nascer *m* do sol
sunset pôr-do-sol *m*
sunstroke insolação *f*; **to get sunstroke**
pegar uma insolação
supermarket supermercado *m* **43**, **83**
sure seguro *m*/segura *f*
surf *(v)* fazer surfe
surfboard prancha *f* de surfe
surfing surfe *m*; **to go surfing** surfar
surname sobrenome *m*, nome *m* de família
surprise *(n)* surpresa *f*
surprise *(v)* surpreender
swallow engolir
swearword palavrão *m*
sweat *(n)* suor *m*
sweat *(v)* suar

sweet *(adj/n)* doce
swelling inchaço *m*
swim *(v)* nadar; **to go for a swim** ir nadar
swimming natação *f*; **swimming pool**
piscina *f*
swimsuit traje *m* de banho
switch off desligar
switch on ligar
switchboard operator telefonista *mf*
swollen inchado *m*/inchada *f*
syrup *(medicine)* xarope *m*

T

table mesa *f* **47**, **48**
tablespoon colher *f* de sopa
tablet comprimido *m*
take *(carry)* levar; *(photos)* bater; *(taxi, train)*
pegar; **it takes two hours** demora duas
horas
take off *(plane)* decolar, levantar vôo
talk falar
tall alto *m*/alta *f*
tampon absorvente *m* interno
tanned bronzeado *m*/bronzeada *f*
tap torneira *f*
taste *(n)* sabor *m*
taste *(v)* provar
tax taxa *f*
taxi táxi *m* **33**; **taxi driver** taxista *mf*
tea chá *m*
teach ensinar
teacher professor(a)
team time *m*
teaspoon colher *f* de chá
teenager adolescente *mf*
telephone *(n)* telefone *m*
telephone *(v)* telefonar
television televisão *f*
tell dizer a
temperature temperatura *f*; **to have a**
temperature ter febre
tennis tênis *m*; **tennis court** quadra *f* de tênis
tent barraca *f*
terminal terminal *m*
terraces *(football)* arquibancada *f*
terrible terrível
text *(SMS)* torpedo *m*
thank agradecer; **thank you** obrigado
m/obrigada *f*; **thank you very much** muito
obrigado/obrigada

thanks obrigado *m*/obrigada *f*; **thanks to** graças a

that aquilo

that *(conj)* que; **I think that ...** acho que ...

that (one) *(adj/pron)* esse *m*/essa *f*; **that book** esse livro

the *(singular)* o *m*/a *f*; *(plural)* os *mpl*/as *fpl*

theatre teatro *m*

theft roubo *m*

their deles *mpl*/delas *fpl*; **their car** o carro deles/delas; **their friends** os amigos deles/delas

theirs deles *mpl*/delas *fpl*; **a friend of theirs** um amigo deles/delas; **it's theirs** é deles/delas; **theirs are here** os/as deles/delas estão aqui

them *(direct object)* os *mpl*/as *fpl*; *(indirect object)* lhes; *(after preposition)* eles *mpl*/elas *fpl*; **I know them** eu os/as conheço; **I don't know them** não os/as conheço; **I asked them** perguntei a eles/elas; **for them** para eles/elas; **it's them** são eles/elas

themselves *(reflexive)* se; *(after preposition)* si; **they didn't hurt themselves** eles/elas não se machucaram

then *(afterwards)* depois

there ali; **there is no space** não tem espaço; **there she is** lá está ela

there is/there are tem, há

therefore por conseguinte

thermometer termômetro *m*

these estes *mpl*/estas *fpl*; **these ones** estes/estas

they eles *mpl*/elas *fpl*; **they say that ...** dizem que ...

thief ladrão *m*/ladra *f*

thigh coxa *f*

thin magro *m*/magra *f*

thing coisa *f*; **things** as coisas; **where are my things?** onde estão as minhas coisas?

think pensar; **to think about** pensar em

thirst sede *f*

thirsty: to be thirsty ter sede

this este *m*/esta *f*; **this one** este/esta; **this evening** esta noite; **this is** isto é

those esses *mpl*/essas *fpl*; **those ones** esses/essas

thread linha *f*

throat garganta *f*; **throat lozenge** pastilha *f* para a garganta

through através de

throw atirar; **to throw away/out** jogar fora

thunderstorm trovoada *f*

Thursday quinta-feira *f*

ticket *(for travel)* passagem *f* **23**; *(for match)* ingresso *m* **78**; *(for theatre, museum)* entrada *f* **67, 73**; **ticket office** bilheteria *f*

tidy arrumado *m*/arrumada *f*

tie gravata *f*

tight apertado *m*/apertada *f*

tights meia-calça *f*

time tempo *m*; *(on clock)* horas *fpl*; *(occasion)* vez *f*; **what time is it?** que horas são?; **from time to time** de vez em quando; **on time** a horas; **three times** três vezes

timetable horário *m* **23**

tinfoil papel *m* de alumínio

tired cansado *m*/cansada *f*

tiring cansativo *m*/cansativa *f*

tissue paper lenço *m* de papel

to *(prep)* a

tobacco tabaco *m*

tobacconist's tabacaria *f*

today hoje

toe dedo *m* do pé

together juntos *mpl*/juntas *fpl*; **we're together** viemos juntos/juntas; **all together** *(everything)* tudo junto

toilet toalete *m* **7**; **toilet bag** nécessaire *f*; **toilet paper** papel *m* higiênico

toiletries artigos *mpl* de toilette

toilets sanitários *mpl* **48**

toll pedágio *m*

tomorrow amanhã; **tomorrow evening** amanhã à noite; **tomorrow morning** amanhã de manhã

tongue língua *f*

tonight hoje à noite

too muito *m*/muita *f*; *(also)* também; **too many** muitos *mpl*/muitas *fpl*; **too much** muito; **it's too hot** está quente demais; **me too** eu também

tooth dente *m*

toothache dor *f* de dente

toothbrush escova *f* de dentes

toothpaste pasta *f* de dentes

top *(n)* *(highest point)* topo *m*; **at the top** no topo

torch lanterna *f*

touch tocar

tour visita f; **tour guide** guia mf

tourism turismo m

tourist turista mf; (adj) turístico m/turística f; **tourist office** posto m de informações turísticas

tow rebocar; **on tow** a reboque

towards para, na direção de; **she turned towards me** ela se virou para mim

towel toalha f

town cidade f; **town centre** centro m da cidade; **town hall** câmara f municipal

toy brinquedo m

traditional tradicional

traffic trânsito m; **traffic jam** engarrafamento m; **traffic lights** semáforo m

train trem m **28**

trainers tênis mpl

transfer (n) (of money) transferência f

translate traduzir

travel viajar; **travel agency** agência f de viagens

traveller viajante mf

traveller's cheque cheque m de viagem

tray tabuleiro m

tree árvore f

trip viagem f; **have a good trip!** boa viagem!

trolley carrinho m

trousers calças fpl

true verdadeiro m/verdadeira f

try (attempt) tentar; (food, clothes) provar **87**; **to try to do something** procurar fazer algo

tube metrô m; **tube station** estação f do metrô

Tuesday terça-feira f

turn (n) (go) vez f; **it's your turn** é a sua vez

turn (v) virar; **to turn back** dar a volta

turn on (light) acender; (machine) ligar; (tap) abrir

turn off (light) apagar; (machine) desligar; (tap) fechar

tweezers pinça f

twice duas vezes fpl

twin room quarto m duplo com duas camas

twist torcer

type (n) tipo m, gênero m

type (v) escrever

typical típico m/típica f

tyre pneu m

U

ugly feio m/feia f

umbrella guarda-chuva m

uncomfortable desconfortável

under (beneath) debaixo (de)

underground metrô m **28**; **underground line** linha f do metrô; **underground station** estação f do metrô

underpants cuecas fpl

understand entender **9**

underwear roupa f de baixo

unforgettable inesquecível

United Kingdom Reino Unido m

United States Estados Unidos mpl

unleaded petrol gasolina f comum

unpleasant desagradável

until até; **until tomorrow** até amanhã

upset transtornado m/transtornada f

urgent urgente

us nos; (after preposition) nós; **he knows us** ele nos conhece; **she didn't ask us** ela não perguntou para nós; **for us** para nós; **with us** conosco

use (v) utilizar, usar; **to be used for** servir para; **I'm used to it** estou acostumado m/acostumada f

used usado m/usada f

useful útil

useless inútil

user usuário m

usually habitualmente

U-turn meia volta f

V

vacant livre

vaccinated (against) vacinado m/vacinada f (contra)

valid válido m/válida f

validity validade f

valley vale m

value valor m

VAT IVA m

vegetable legume m

vegetarian vegetariano m/vegetariana f

vehicle viatura f

very muito; **very happy** muito contente

video vídeo m

view vista f; **with a sea view** com vista para o mar

viewpoint mirador m

village aldeia f

visa visto m; **entry/exit visa** visto de

entrada/saída
visit (n) visita f
visit (v) visitar
visitor visita mf
voice voz f
volleyball vôlei m
voltage voltagem f
vomit (v) vomitar
voucher vale m

W

waist cintura f
wait esperar; **to wait for somebody/
something** esperar alguém/algo
waiter garçom m
waitress garçonete f
wake up acordar
Wales País de Gales m
walk (v) andar; (leisurely) passear
walk (n) passeio m
wall (external) muro m; (internal) parede f
wallet carteira f (de documentos)
want querer; **to want to do something**
querer fazer alguma coisa
warm quente
warn avisar
wash lavar; **to wash one's hair** lavar a
cabeça
washbasin pia f
washing: washing machine máquina f de
lavar roupa; **washing powder** sabão m
em pó
washing-up liquid detergente m para a louça
waste (n) lixo m
waste (v) perder; **to waste time** perder
tempo
watch (n) relógio m (de pulso)
watch (v) (observe) ver; (look after) tomar
conta (de); **watch out!** cuidado!
water água f; **water heater** aquecedor m
de água
waterproof à prova d'água, impermeável
waterskiing esqui m aquático
wave onda f
way (route) caminho m **11**; (direction) direção
m; (manner) maneira f; **this way, please**
por aqui, por favor; **way in** entrada f; **way
out** saída f
we nós
weak fraco m/fraca f

wear (clothes) vestir; (shoes) calçar; (glasses,
perfume) usar
weather tempo m; **the weather's good/
bad** o tempo está bom/ruim; **weather
forecast** previsão f do tempo
website site m
wedding casamento m
Wednesday quarta-feira f
week semana f
weekend fim m de semana
welcome bem-vindo m/bem-vinda f;
welcome! bem-vindos!; **you're welcome**
de nada!
well bem; **I'm very well** estou bem; **to get
on well with someone** dar-se bem com
alguém; **well done** (meat) bem-passado
m/bem-passada f
well-known conhecido m/conhecida f
Welsh galês m/galesa f
west oeste m; **in the west** no oeste; **(to
the) west of** a oeste de
wet molhado m/molhada f
wetsuit roupa f de mergulho
what o que; **what do you want?** o que
deseja?; **what is it?** o que é?
wheel (of car, bike) roda f; (steering wheel)
volante m
wheelchair cadeira f de rodas
when quando
where onde; **where is/are ...?** onde
está/estão ...?; **where are you from?** de
onde você é?; **where are you going?** para
onde vocês vão?
which (o) qual/(os) quais, que
while enquanto; **while he ate** enquanto ele
comia; **wait a while** espere um momento;
in a while daqui a pouco
white branco m/branca f
who quem; **who's calling?** quem é?
whose (one) cujo m/cuja fpl; (more than one)
cujos mpl/cujas fpl; **whose ...?** de quem ...?
why por que; **why?** por quê?; **that is why ...**
é por isso que ...
wide largo m/larga f
widow viúva f
widower viúvo m
wife esposa f
wild selvagem
win ganhar
wind vento m

window janela f; **in the window** na janela; **to go window-shopping** ver vitrines
windscreen pára-brisa m
windsurfing windsurfe m; **to go windsurfing** fazer windsurfe
wine vinho m; **wine list** carta f de vinhos
winner vencedor(a)
winter inverno m
will vontade f; **against one's will** contra a vontade
with com
withdraw (money) sacar
withdrawal (of money) saque m
without sem
woman mulher f
wonderful lindo m/linda f
wood madeira f
wool lã f
word palavra f
work (n) trabalho m; **work of art** obra f de arte
work (v) trabalhar; (machine) funcionar **100**
world mundo m
worry (n) preocupação f
worry: don't worry não se preocupe
worse, worst pior; **to get worse** piorar; **it's worse (than)** é pior (do que)
worth: to be worth valer a pena; **it's worth it** vale a pena
wound ferida f

wrap embrulhar
wrist pulso m
write escrever **85**
wrong errado m/errada f

X

X-ray raio m X , radiografia f

Y

year ano m
yellow amarelo m/amarela f
yes sim
yesterday ontem; **yesterday evening** ontem à noite
yet ainda; **not yet** ainda não
you você (see grammar)
young jovem, novo m/nova f
your seu m/sua f (see grammar)
yours o(s) seu(s) m/a(s) sua(s) f (see grammar)
youth hostel albergue m da juventude

Z

zero zero m
zip zíper m
zoo jardim m zoológico

DICTIONARY

PORTUGUESE-ENGLISH

A

a (prep) to; (time) at

a (pron) her, it; **as** them; **eu a/as conheço** I know her/them; see grammar

a(s) (art) the; see grammar

abacaxi pineapple

abadia abbey

abaixo down; **rua/escadas abaixo** down the street/stairs; **abaixo de** below

abelha bee

aberto/a open

abridor de latas can opener

abril April

abrir to open

absorvente: absorvente higiênico sanitary towel; **absorvente interno** tampon

acabar to finish; to end up

acampar to go camping; to camp

acaso: por acaso by chance; **ao acaso** at random

aceitar to accept

acender (candle, cigarette) to light

achar to find

acidente accident

acima up; **acima de** above; **acima de tudo** above all; **rua acima** up the street

acompanhar to accompany

aconselhar to advise

acontecer to happen

acordar to wake up

açougue butcher's

acreditar to believe

adaptador adaptor

adeus goodbye

adiantado (adv) in advance

adoecer to fall ill

adolescente teenager

adorar to love (to)

adulto/a adult

advogado/a lawyer

aeroporto airport

afogar-se to drown

agência de viagens travel agency

agora now

agosto August

agradar: agradar a to please; **não me agrada** I don't like it

agradável pleasant

agradecer to thank

água water; **água potável** drinking water

agulha needle

aguardar to wait; **aguardar alguém** to wait for someone

ainda still; yet; **ainda falta um** one is still missing; **ainda não** not yet; **ainda bem** just as well

ajuda help

ajudar to help

albergue da juventude youth hostel

álcool alcohol; **sem álcool** non-alcoholic

aldeia village

alérgico/a allergic

alfândega customs

algas seaweed

algodão cotton

alguém somebody, someone

algum/alguma some; **alguma coisa** something

alguns/algumas some; **algumas pessoas** some people

ali there; over there; **é por ali** it's that way

almoçar to have lunch

almoço lunch

almofada pillow

almofadinha cushion

alô hello (on phone)

alojamento accommodation

alojar to put someone up

alto/a high; tall; (noise) loud

alugar to rent, to hire; **alugar a** to rent out to

aluga-se for rent, for hire

aluguel rent

amanhã tomorrow; **amanhã de manhã/à noite** tomorrow morning/evening

amarelo/a yellow

amargo/a bitter

ambiente atmosphere; environment

ambos/as both
ambulância ambulance
americano/a American
amigo/a friend
amor love
analgésico painkiller
andar *(n)* floor
andar *(v)* to walk; **andar de bicicleta** to cycle
anel ring
anestesia anaesthetic
animação buzz, lively atmosphere
animado/a lively, busy
animal animal
aniversário anniversary; birthday; **feliz aniversário** happy birthday
ano year; **Ano Novo** New Year; **quantos anos você tem?** how old are you?
antecipado in advance
anteontem the day before yesterday
anterior previous
antes (de) before
antibiótico antibiotic
anticoncepcional contraceptive; pill; **tomar anticoncepcional** to be on the pill
antigo/a old; ancient
antigüidade antique
apagar to delete; to put out
aparelhagem hi-fi system
apartamento flat
apenas only, just; **apenas um** just one
apendicite appendicitis
apertado/a tight
apertar to press
apoiar to support; **apoiar em** to rest against
apontar para to point at
aposentado/a retired
aprender to learn
apresentar to present; **apresentar alguém a alguém** to introduce someone to someone
aproveitar-se de to take advantage of
aquecedor heater; **aquecedor eléctrico/a gás** electric/gas heater; **aquecedor de água** water heater
aquecimento heating
aquele/a that; that one
aqui here; **aqui é David** *(on phone)* this is David (speaking); **aqui está/estão** here is/are; **até aqui** up to now; **daqui a pouco**

in a little while; **por aqui, por favor** this way, please
aquilo that
ar air; **ao ar livre** in the open air
ar-condicionado air conditioning
árbitro referee
aranha spider
área area
areia sand
armazém store
arquibancada *(in stadium)* terraces
arquivo file
arranha-céus skyscraper
arrebentar to burst
arroba at sign
arrombar to break into
arrumado/a tidy
arte art
artesanato handicraft
artigo article
artista artist
árvore tree
asma asthma
aspirina aspirin
assalto robbery
assim like this; **assim assim** so-so; **assim que** as soon as
assinar to sign
assinatura signature
atacar to attack
atadura bandage
atalho short cut
ataque attack; **ataque cardíaco** heart attack
até *(time)* until; *(distance)* as far as; *(height, quantity)* up to; **até amanhã** see you tomorrow; **até mais** see you soon; **até mais tarde** see you later; **até o pescoço** up to the neck
atenção attention; **atenção!** look out!
atender to serve; *(on phone)* to reply
atirar to throw; *(with gun)* to shoot
atrás (de) behind; **... atrás** ... ago
atrasado/a delayed; late
atraso delay
através through; by way of
atravessar to cross
atrevido/a forward
atropelado/a: ser atropelado/a to be run over
auditório concert hall

aula lesson
auto-estrada motorway
automóvel car; **de automóvel** by car
avaria breakdown
ave bird
avenida avenue
avião aeroplane; **por avião** by air/airmail
avisar to warn
aviso notice; warning
azeite (olive) oil
azul blue; **azul-claro** light blue; **azul-escuro** dark blue

B

bagagem luggage; **bagagem de mão** hand luggage
baile dance
bairro area, neighbourhood, quarter
baixar to lower; (file) to download
baixo (adv) (speak, laugh) quietly; **no andar de baixo** downstairs; **em/por baixo de** under(neath)
baixo/a (adj) low; short
balão balloon
balcão counter; bar
balé ballet
balsa ferry
banca (de jornais) newsagent
banco stool; seat; (for money) bank; (in hospital) casualty; **banco de jardim** bench
Band-Aid® sticking plaster
banda band
bandeira flag
banheira bathtub
banheiro toilet; bathroom; **banheiro privativo** ensuite bathroom
banho bath; **tomar banho** to have a bath/a shower; (in sea, river) to have a swim
bar bar
baralho pack of cards
barata (n) cockroach
barato/a cheap
barba beard; **fazer a barba** to shave
barbeador elétrico electric shaver
barbear-se to shave
barco boat
barraca tent
barriga belly; **barriga da perna** calf
barro clay; mud; **de barro** earthenware
barroco/a baroque

barulhento/a noisy
barulho noise
basquete basketball
bastante a lot, plenty; **bastante dinheiro** a lot of money
batedor de carteira pickpocket
bater (photos) to take
bateria battery
bebê baby
bêbado/a drunk
beber to drink
bebida drink
beijar to kiss
beijo kiss
beira-mar seaside; **à beira-mar** by the sea
belo/a beautiful
bem well; **está bem!** OK!, all right!; **tudo bem?** all right?; **estou bem** I'm fine; **fez bem!** you did the right thing!
bem-vindo/a welcome
biblioteca library
bicicleta bike
bigode moustache
bilhete (air) ticket
bilheteria ticket office; box office
binóculos binoculars
biológico/a organic
boa see **bom**
boas-vindas welcome; **dar as boas vindas a alguém** to welcome someone
boca mouth
bóia buoy
bola ball
bolha blister
bolso pocket
bom/boa good; **bom dia** good morning; **boa tarde** good afternoon; **boa noite** good evening
bomba: bomba (de bicicleta) bicycle pump; **bomba (de gasolina)** petrol station
bombeiros fire brigade
boné cap
bonito/a pretty
bosque woods
bota boots
botão button
botequim pub, tavern
botijão de gás gas cylinder
braço arm
branco/a white

Brasil Brazil
brasileiro/a Brazilian
breve brief; **em breve** soon; **até breve** see you soon
briga fight
brincar to play
brincos earrings
brinquedo toy
brochura brochure
bronquite bronchitis
bronzeado (n) tan
bronzeado/a tanned
bronzear-se to get a tan
bufê self-service restaurant; **bufê livre** fixed-price buffet
buraco hole
buscar to look for; **ir buscar algo** to fetch something; **ir buscar alguém** to pick someone up

C

cabeça head
cabeleireiro/a hairdresser
cabelo hair
cabide coathanger
cabine (phone) box; (photo) booth
cabra goat
caçarola saucepan
cacete stick; (bread) baguette
cachaça white sugar-cane rum
cachecol scarf
cachorro-quente hot-dog
cada each; **cada um(a)** each one; **a cada dois dias** every other day
cadeia prison
cadeira chair; seat; **cadeira de rodas** wheelchair
caderno notebook
café (drink) coffee; (place) café; **café preto/com leite** black/white coffee; **café da manhã** breakfast
caiaque kayak
caipirinha cocktail of cachaça rum with lime juice
cair to fall
cais (de embarque) quay
caixa box; (in shop) checkout; (in bank) cashier; **caixa automático** cashpoint; **caixa de câmbio** gearbox; **caixa de correio** postbox; **caixa de entrada/saída** inbox/outbox

caixote box
calçar to put on; **calço ...** I take size ... shoes
calças trousers; **calças de brim** jeans
calções shorts; **calções-de-banho** swimming trunks
calmo/a calm; quiet
calor heat; **estar com calor** to feel hot; **está calor** it's hot
cama bed; **cama de casal** double bed; **cama de solteiro** single bed
camada layer
câmara municipal town hall
câmera (fotográfica) camera; **câmera digital** digital camera; **câmera de vídeo** camcorder
câmbio currency exchange; exchange rate
caminhão lorry
caminhar to walk
caminho way; path; **a/no caminho** on the way
camisa shirt
camisinha condom
camisola jumper
camping campsite; **fazer camping** to go camping
campo countryside; field; **campo de futebol** football pitch; **campo de golfe** golf course; **campo de tênis** tennis court
canal channel; canal
canção song
cancelar to cancel
candeeiro lamp
caneta pen
cano pipe
canoagem canoeing; **fazer canoagem** to go canoeing
cansaço tiredness
cansado/a tired
cansativo/a tiring
cantar to sing
cantil water bottle; flask
cão dog
capa de chuva raincoat
capacete helmet
capela chapel
cara face; guy
caravana caravan
cardápio menu
cárie: ter uma cárie to have a decayed tooth
caro/a dear, expensive

caroço stone

carona: pegar carona/viajar de carona to hitchhike

carregar to carry

carrinho trolley; **carrinho de bebê** pram, pushchair

carro car; **de carro** by car

carruagem coach, carriage

carta letter; (playing) card; **carta registrada** recorded letter; **carta de vinhos** wine list

cartão card; **cartão de crédito** credit card; **cartão de débito** debit card; **cartão de sócio** membership card; **cartão telefônico** phonecard; **(cartão-)postal** postcard

cartaz poster; **estar em cartaz** (show, film) to be showing

carteira wallet; licence; card; **carteira de motorista** driving licence; **carteira de estudante** student card

carteiro postman

casa house; **em casa** at home; **ir para casa** to go home; **casa de câmbio** bureau de change

casaco jacket; cardigan

casado/a married

casamento wedding

caseiro/a homemade

caso: em caso de in case of

castanho/a brown

castelo castle

catedral cathedral

católico/a Catholic

catorze fourteen

causa cause; **por causa de** because of

cavalo horse

cedo soon; early; **é muito cedo** it's too soon

cego/a blind

celular cellphone, mobile

cemitério cemetery

centímetro centimetre

centro centre; **centro comercial** shopping centre; **centro da cidade** town centre; **centro de saúde** clinic

CEP postcode

cerca: cerca de about, around

certo/a correct; certain

céu sky

chá tea

chamada call

chamar to call; **chamar-se** to be called

chão floor; ground; **no chão** on the floor

chapa elétrica hotplate

chapéu hat

charuto cigar

chato/a boring

chave key

chefe boss

chegada arrival

chegar to arrive; to be enough; **já chega!** that's enough!

cheio/a full

cheirar to smell; **cheirar bem/mal** to smell good/bad

cheiro smell

cheque cheque; **cheque de viagem** traveller's cheque

chiclete chewing gum

chinelos (de quarto) slippers

chocante shocking

chocolate chocolate

chope draught beer

choque shock; crash

chover to rain; **está chovendo** it's raining

chumbo lead

chupeta dummy

churrascaria barbecue restaurant

churrasco barbecue (meat)

chuva rain

chuveiro shower

cibercafé Internet café, cybercafé

cicatrizar to heal

ciclovia cycle path

cidade city

cigarro cigarette

cima: em cima de on, on top of; **por cima de** over, above; **parte de cima** upper part

cinema cinema

cinemateca filmhouse

cinto belt; **cinto de segurança** seatbelt

cintura waist

cinzeiro ashtray

cinzento/a grey

circo circus

circuito turístico tourist trail

circulação circulation

claro/a (adj) light; (sky) clear

claro (adv) clear; **é claro!** of course!

classe class; **classe econômica** economy class; **classe executiva** business class

clima climate

clínico geral GP
clube club; **clube noturno** nightclub
cobertor blanket
cobrar to charge
cobrir to cover
coçar to itch
código code; **código pessoal** PIN (number);
  código postal postcode
coelho rabbit
cofre safe deposit box
coisa thing
cola glue
colar *(n)* necklace
colar *(v)* to glue; *(text)* to paste
colchão mattress
coleção collection
coleta (mail) collection
colher spoon
colina hill
colônia colony; *(perfume)* cologne
colônia de férias summer camp
colorido *(film)* colour
com with
começar to begin
comer to eat
comerciante shopkeeper
comércio commerce
comida food
comissão commission
como like; as; how; **bem como** as well as;
  como você está? how are you?
companhia company; **companhia aérea**
  airline
compartimento compartment
completo/a complete; full
comprar to buy
compras shopping; **fazer as compras** to
  do the shopping; **ir fazer compras** to go
  shopping
compreender to understand
comprido/a long
comprimido *(n)* tablet; **comprimido para
  as dores** painkiller
comprovante receipt
computador computer
concerto concert
concha seashell
concordar to agree
condimentado/a spicy
conduzir to drive

conectar-se to go online
confiança trust
confiar: confiar algo a alguém to entrust
  someone with something
confirmar to confirm
confortável comfortable
congelado/a frozen
congelador freezer
conhecer to know
conhecido/a *(adj)* well-known
conjunto set; *(musical)* band, group
conseguir: conseguir fazer to manage to do
conselho advice
construído/a built
construir to build
consulado consulate
consulta appointment
conta bill; **tomar conta de** to take care of;
  conta (bancária) bank account
contato contact; **entrar em contato com**
  to contact
contador meter
contagioso/a contagious
contar to count; **contar com** to count on
contente happy
continuação continuation
continuar to continue
contra against
contrário/a opposite; **na direção
  contrária/no sentido contrário** in the
  opposite direction
contrato contract
convidar to invite
cópia copy
copiar to copy
copo glass; **um copo de água** a glass of water
cor colour
coração heart
cordeiro lamb
cor-de-laranja orange
cor-de-rosa pink
corpo body
corredor de ônibus bus lane
correto/a correct
correio mail, post; *(building)* post office; **pelo
  correio** by post; **correio aéreo** airmail;
  correio eletrônico e-mail
corrente current; chain
correr to run
correspondência correspondence

cortar to cut; **cortar-se** to cut oneself
cortador de unha nail clippers
cortiça cork
costa coast
costas back
costela rib
cotonete cotton bud
couro leather
coxa thigh
cozinha kitchen; **com cozinha** (accommodation) self-catering
cozinhar to cook
creme cream; **creme de barbear** shaving cream; **creme hidratante** moisturizer; **creme solar** sun cream
crer: crer que to believe that
crescer to grow
criança child
crise crisis
cru(a) raw
cruz cross
cruzamento junction; crossroads
cruzeiro cruise
cubo de gelo ice cube
cueca underpants; knickers
cuidado; cuidado! watch out!; **cuidado com …** beware of …; **com cuidado** carefully
cuidar: cuidar de to look after
cujo/a whose
cume summit
curar to cure
curativo dressing
curso course
curto/a short
custar to cost

D

dados details; data
dança dance
dançar to dance
danificado/a damaged
daqui from here; **daqui a um mês** in a month's time; **daqui em diante** from now on; **daqui a pouco** in a little while
dar to give; **dar problema** to create problems; **dar para a praia** to look out onto the beach
data date; **data de nascimento** date of birth; **data de validade/vencimento**
expiry date
de of; **de carro** by car; **de preto** in black; **de São Paulo** from São Paulo; **mais lento do que** slower than; **de … a …** from … to …
debaixo (de) under, underneath; **por debaixo de** below
decepcionante disappointing
decidir to decide
declaração statement
declarar to declare
dedo finger; **dedo do pé** toe
defeito flaw
deficiente disabled
degrau step
deitar-se to lie down; to go to bed
deixar to let; to leave
delegacia (de polícia) police station
dele/dela its; his; her; hers; **a bagagem dele** his luggage; **um amigo dela** a friend of hers
deles/delas their; theirs; **o carro deles** their car; **um amigo deles** a friend of theirs
demais too; too much; too many; **está quente demais** it's too hot; **tem água demais** there's too much water
demasiado/a too; too much; too many
demora delay
dentada bite
dente tooth
dentista dentist
dentro inside; **dentro do armário** in the wardrobe; **dentro em pouco** soon; **dentro de uma hora** in an hour
departamento department
depender (de) to depend (on)
depois then; afterwards; later; **depois de** after; **depois do almoço** after lunch
depósito deposit; **depósito de bagagem** left-luggage (office)
depressa quickly; **depressa!** hurry up!
desagradável unpleasant
desaparecer to disappear
desastre disaster; accident
descansar to rest
descarregar to unload; (on computer) to download
descartável disposable
descascar to peel
descer (hill) to go down; (bus) to get off; (price, level) to fall, to decrease
descobrir to discover; to find out

decolar *(aircraft)* to take off
desconfortável uncomfortable
desconto discount; concession
desculpa excuse
desculpar-se to excuse oneself; **desculpe, ...** excuse me, ...; **desculpe!** sorry!
desde since; **desde que** as long as
desejo desire; wish
desenho drawing
desinfetar to disinfect
desistir de to give up
desligar to switch off; *(telephone)* to hang up
desmaiar to faint
desodorante deodorant
despertador alarm clock
destinatário/a addressee
detergente para louça washing-up liquid
detestar to hate
devagar slowly
dever *(n)* duty
dever *(v)* must; should; to owe; **deve ser cinco horas** it must be 5 o'clock; **deve fazer sol amanhã** it should be sunny tomorrow; **dever algo a alguém** to owe something to someone
devolver to give back; to return
dezembro December
dia day
diabetes diabetes
diante de in front of, before
dicionário dictionary
dieta diet; **estar de dieta** to be on a diet; **entrar em dieta** to go on a diet
diferença difference; **diferença no fuso horário** time difference
diferente (de) different (from)
difícil difficult
digitar *(data)* to enter
diminuir to decrease
dinheiro money; **dinheiro vivo** hard cash; **dinheiro trocado** small change; **trocar dinheiro** to change money; **pagar em dinheiro** to pay cash
direção direction; **na direção de** towards
direto/a direct
direito *(n)* right; **ter o direito de ...** to have the right to ...
direito/a *(adj)* right; **à direita** on the right; **à direita de** to the right of; **do lado direito** on the right

discar to dial
disco disk; record
discoteca disco; club
discutir to discuss
disponível spare; available
disso: nada disso nothing like that
DIU coil
divertido/a funny; enjoyable; entertaining
divertir-se to enjoy oneself
divorciado/a divorced
dizer to say, to tell
doce sweet
documento document; **documento de identificação** ID
doença illness
doente *(adj)* ill
doente *(n)* patient
doer to hurt; **me dói o/a ...** I have a sore ...
doido/a mad
domingo Sunday
dono/a owner
dor pain; **dor de cabeça** headache; **dor de dente** toothache; **dor de estômago** stomach ache; **dor nas costas** backache
dormir to sleep
doutor(a) doctor
drinque *(alcoholic)* drink
drogaria drug store, pharmacy
droga drugs
ducha shower
duração duration
durante during
durar to last
Durex® Sellotape®
duro/a hard

e and
edifício building
educado/a polite
ele/ela he; she; it; **é ele/ela** it's him/her
eletricidade electricity
elétrico/a *(adj)* electric
eletrônico/a electronic
eles/elas they; **são eles/elas** it's them
elevador lift, elevator
em in; on; at; **em São Paulo** in São Paulo; **no domingo** on Sunday; **no hotel** at the hotel
e-mail e-mail; e-mail address
embaixada embassy

embarcar to board
embarque boarding
embora even though; **ir embora** to go away
embreagem clutch
embriagado/a drunk
embrulhar to wrap; **embrulhar para presente** to gift-wrap
embrulho parcel
emergência emergency; **em caso de emergência** in case of emergency; **emergência** casualty (department)
empregado/a employee; **empregada doméstica** maid
emprego job
emprestar to lend
empurrar to push
encher to fill
encomenda order; request
encontrar to find; **encontrar-se** to meet
encontro appointment; **marcar um encontro** to make an appointment; **ter um encontro (com)** to have an appointment (with)
endereço address
enfermeiro/a nurse
enfim at last
enganar-se to make a mistake
engarrafamento traffic jam
engolir to swallow
engraçado/a funny
enjoado/a sick, queasy
enquanto while
ensinar to teach
então so; well
entender to understand
entrada admission (ticket); entrance, way in
entrar to come in; to go in
entre among; between
envelope envelope
enviar to send
epiléptico/a epileptic
equipe team
equipamento equipment
equitação horse riding
errado/a wrong
erro mistake
escadas stairs
escalada climbing; **fazer uma escalada** to go climbing
escocês/esa Scottish

Escócia Scotland
escola school
escolha choice
escolher to choose
escova brush; **escova de dentes** toothbrush
escrever to write; to type
escultura sculpture
escuro/a dark; *(sky)* overcast
esforço effort; **fazer um esforço** to make an effort
esgotado/a sold out
eslaide slide
especial special
especialidade speciality
espetacular great, wonderful
espetáculo show
espelho mirror; **espelho retrovisor** rearview mirror
esperar to hope; to wait; **espero que** I hope that; **espere aqui um momento** wait here a moment
espinha spot
esponja sponge
esporte sport
esposa wife
espuma de barbear shaving foam
esquecer-se (de) to forget
esquerdo/a left; **à esquerda** on the left; **à esquerda de** to the left of
esqui aquático waterskiing
esquina corner
esse/essa that; **esse livro** that book
esses/essas those; those ones
estaca tent peg
estação station; **estação de rádio** radio station; **estação do ano** season; **estação do metrô** tube station; **estação rodoviária** bus station; **estação balneária** seaside resort
estacionamento parking, car park
estacionar to park
estadia stay; **boa estadia!** enjoy your stay!
estádio stadium
estado state
estado civil married status
Estados Unidos United States
estágio traineeship
estar to be; **está frio** it's cold; **como você está?** how are you?; **estar com dor de ...** to have a sore ...

estátua statue

este/esta this; this one; **esta noite** this evening

estepe spare tyre

estes/estas these; these ones

estilo style

estômago stomach

estrada road

estragar to spoil

estrangeiro/a *(adj)* foreign; **no estrangeiro** abroad

estrangeiro/a *(n)* foreigner

estranho/a strange

estuário estuary

estudante student

estudar to study

estudo study

eu I; me; **eu sou inglês** I'm English; **sou eu** it's me

euro euro

Europa Europe

europeu/éia European

excelente excellent

excepcional exceptional

exceto except

excesso excess; **ter excesso de peso** to be overweight; **excesso de bagagem** excess luggage

excursão excursion

exemplo example; **por exemplo** for example

êxito success

experimentar to try; to try on

explicar to explain

exposição exhibition

expressão expression

expresso/a express; **por correio expresso** by express post

exterior outside

extra extra

extraordinário/a extraordinary

F

faca knife

face face

fácil easy

falar to speak; to talk

falhar to fail

falso/a false, fake

faltar to miss; **faltam duas pessoas** there are two people missing

família family

farmácia chemist's, drugstore; **farmácia 24 horas** duty chemist's

farol lighthouse

farol dianteiro headlight

farto: estar farto de to be fed up with

fatia slice

fato fact; **de fato** indeed

fatura invoice; bill

favor favour; **fazer um favor a alguém** to do someone a favour; **por favor** please

favorito/a favourite

faz ago; **faz muito tempo** a long time ago

fazenda ranch

fazer to make; to do; **fazer fila** to queue

febre fever, (high) temperature; **estar com febre** to have a temperature

fechado/a closed

fechadura lock

fechar to shut, to close; **fechar à chave** to lock

fecho zip

feio/a ugly

feira street market; **feira popular** funfair

feliz happy

feriado public holiday; **feriado nacional** national holiday

férias holiday(s); **de férias** on holiday

ferida *(n)* wound

ferido/a *(adj)* injured

ferro de passar iron

festa party

festejar to celebrate

festival festival

fevereiro February

ficar to stay; to be; **fica bem em você** it suits you

ficha form

fígado liver

fila queue; **fazer fila** to queue; **furar a fila** to jump the queue

filha daughter

filho son

filme film, movie; *(for camera)* roll of film

fim end; **no fim de** at the end of; **fim de semana** weekend

fio cable

fita cassete cassette tape

fino/a fine; thin

flor flower

floresta forest
fogão stove; **fogão de acampamento** camping stove
fogo fire; **tem fogo?** do you have a light; **fogo de artifício** fireworks
folha leaf; **folha de papel** sheet of paper; **folha de alumínio** tinfoil
folheto leaflet
fome hunger; **ter/estar com fome** to be hungry
fora outside; **jantar/almoçar fora** to eat out; **estar fora** to be away; **fora!** get out!; **fora de serviço** out of order/service
forma shape
formiga ant
formulário form
fornecer to provide
forno oven
forte strong
fósforo match
fotocópia photocopy
fotografia photo; **tirar uma fotografia (de)** to take a photo (of)
fraco/a weak
fratura fracture
frágil fragile
fralda nappy
frasco jar; bottle
frase sentence
freio brake; **freio de mão** handbrake
frente front; **em/à frente de** in front of; **para a frente** forward; **reto em frente** straight ahead
fresco/a cool
frigideira frying pan
frigorífico fridge
frio/a cold; chilly; **está frio** it's cold; **tenho/estou com frio** I'm cold
fronha pillowcase
fronteira border
fruta fruit
fuga leak
fumante smoker; **não fumante** non-smoking
fumar to smoke
funcionar to work, to function
fundo (n) bottom; **no fundo (de)** at the bottom (of)
fundo/a (adj) deep
furado/a pierced; punctured; **ter um pneu furado** to have a flat tyre

furar to pierce; to puncture
furo puncture
fusível fuse
futebol football

G

gaivota seagull
galeria de arte gallery
galês/esa Welsh
galinha chicken
galo cockerel
ganhar to win; to earn
garagem garage
garantia guarantee
garfo fork
garganta throat
garrafa bottle
gás gas; **com gás** (drink) sparkling
gasolina petrol; **gasolina comum** unleaded petrol; **gasolina aditivada** four-star petrol
gastar (money) to spend
gato cat
gaze gauze
geada frost
gel de banho shower gel
gelo ice
gêmeo/a twin
gênero type
gente people; **toda gente** everybody; **muita gente** a lot of people
gentil polite
geral general
gerente manager
gerenciar to manage
gesso plaster (cast)
gilete disposable razor
ginecologista gynaecologist
goiaba guava
golfe golf
gordo/a fat
gorjeta tip
gostar de to like; **eu gostaria de ...** I'd like ...; **gosto muito** I like it a lot
gosto taste; **com gosto** with pleasure
gotas drops
graça: de graça free; **graças a** thanks to
grades: ir para atrás das grades to get arrested
grama grass; (weight) gram
grande big

grátis free
gratuito free
grau degree
gravar to record
gravata tie
grave serious
grávida pregnant
gripe cold; **ter gripe** to have a cold; **pegar uma gripe** to catch a cold
gritar to cry
grupo group
guarda policeman
guarda-chuva umbrella
guarda-costeira coastguard
guardanapo napkin; **guardanapo de papel** paper napkin
guardar to keep
guarda-sol parasol
guerra war
guia guide
guichê ticket office

H

há there is/are
hábito habit; **ter o hábito (de)** to be in the habit (of)
handebol handball
Havaianas® flip-flops
hemorróidas piles
hesitar to hesitate
hipermercado hypermarket
história history
hoje today; **hoje em dia** nowadays; **hoje à noite** tonight
hóquei hockey
homem man
homens gents toilets
homossexual homosexual
hora hour; **na hora** on time; **a que horas?** at what time?; **hora local** local time
horário timetable; appointments; **horário de abertura** opening time; **horário de funcionamento** opening hours; **horário de fechamento** closing time
horrível horrible
hóspede guest
hospedado/a: estar hospedado em to be staying at
hospital hospital
hotel hotel

I

ida outward journey
idade age
idéia idea
identificação identity (papers)
idiota stupid
idoso/a elderly
igreja church
igual the same; **para mim é igual** it's all the same to me
ilha island
imóvel still
impermeável waterproof
importância importance; *(money)* amount
importante important
importar-se to mind; **não me importo** I don't mind
imposto alfandegário customs duty
impressão impression; **ter a impressão de que** to have the impression that
impressionante impressive
imprimir to print
incêndio fire
inchaço bump; swelling
inchado/a swollen
incluído/a included; **com tudo incluído** fully inclusive
incomodar to disturb; **não incomodar** *(sign)* do not disturb
incrível incredible
independente independent
indicador indicator
indicativo dialling code
inesquecível unforgettable
infecção infection
informação information
informações directory enquiries
Inglaterra England
inglês/esa English
ingresso ticket *(for match)*
iniciais initials
início beginning; **no início de** at the beginning of
injeção injection
inscrever-se to sign up
inseticida insecticide
inseto insect
inserir to insert; *(number)* to enter
insolação sunstroke; **pegar uma insolação**

to get sunstroke
insônia insomnia
insulto insult
inteiro/a entire; whole
inteligente intelligent
intenção intention; **ter a intenção de** to
have the intention of
intenso/a intense; *(rain)* heavy
interessante interesting
internacional international
intervalo interval; break; half-time
intoxicação alimentar food poisoning
inútil useless
inverno winter
ir to go; **ir a São Paulo** to go to São Paulo; **ir
embora** to go away; **vamos!** let's go!
irmã sister
irmão brother
irritação de pele rash
irritado/a irritated; annoyed
irritar to irritate, to annoy
isqueiro lighter
isso that; **isso!** there you go!; **e é por isso
que** that is why
isto this; **isto é** that is to say
IVA VAT

já already; now; at once; **é para já!** coming
up!; **já esteve em Porto Alegre?** have
you ever been to Porto Alegre?
janeiro January
janela window
jantar *(n)* dinner
jantar *(v)* to have dinner
jardim garden; **jardim botânico** botanical
garden; **jardim zoológico** zoo
jarra jug
joalheria jeweller's
joelho knee
jogar to play; *(object)* to throw; **jogar fora** to
throw away
jogo match; game
jóias jewellery
jornal newspaper
jovem young
juiz judge; referee
julho July

junho June
junto/a together; **tudo junto** all together;
viemos juntos/juntas we are together
justo/a just

lá there; **lá está ela** there she is; **sei lá** I
have no idea
lã wool
lábio lip
lado side; **ao lado de** beside
ladrão/ladra thief
lago lake
lama mud
lamentar to regret; **lamento, mas ...** I'm
sorry, but ...
lâmina de barbear razor blade
lâmpada light bulb
lanche snack
lanterna torch
lápis pencil
laranja orange
lareira fireplace
largo/a wide
lata can
lavandaria launderette
lavandaria a seco dry cleaner's
lavar to wash; **lavar a cabeça** to wash one's
hair; **lavar a roupa** to do the washing;
lavar a louça to do the washing up; **lavar-
se** to have a wash
lavatório lavatory
legendado/a subtitled
legume vegetable
leite milk
lembrança souvenir
lembrar to remind
lembrar-se (de) to remember
lenço; lenço (de mão) handkerchief; **lenço
de papel** tissue paper
lençol sheet
lenha firewood
lente lens; **lentes de contato** contact lenses
lento/a slow
ler to read
leste east; **a leste de** (to the) east of; **no
leste** in the east
letra letter; handwriting
levantar to lift; *(money)* to withdraw
levantar-se to get up; **levantar vôo** to

take off

levar to carry; to take; **leva duas horas** it takes two hours; **para levar** takeaway

leve light

lhe(s) you; it; her; him; them; **eu lhe perguntei** I asked him/her/you; **eu lhes dei** I gave them/you; *see grammar*

ligação call; **fazer uma ligação** to make a call; **ligação a cobrar** reverse-charge call

ligado/a on

ligar to plug in; *(TV, radio)* to switch on; **ligar para** *(phone)* to call

limpar to clean

limpeza cleaning

limpo/a clean

lindo/a beautiful

língua tongue; language

linha line; thread; **linha do metrô** underground line

liquidação sales

líquido/a liquid

lista list; **lista telefônica** phone book

litro litre

livraria bookshop

livre free; vacant

livro book

lixeira bin

lixo waste; rubbish

local de nascimento place of birth

logo later; **até logo** see you later; **logo à noite** this evening; **logo que** as soon as

loja shop; **loja de departamentos** department store

longe far; **longe de** far from; **muito longe** far away

longo/a long

lotação esgotada sold out

lotado/a full

louça dishes

lua moon

lua-de-mel honeymoon

lugar place; seat; **há lugar para a minha mala?** is there room for my suitcase?; **lugar para estacionar** parking space

luva glove

luxo luxury; **de luxo** luxury

luz light

M

maçã apple

machucar to hurt; to bump

madeira wood

mãe mother

magro/a thin; slim

maio May

mais more; plus; **mais de** more than; **muito mais** much more, a lot more; **mais alguma coisa?** would you like anything else?; **mais um/uma ...** one more ...

mal bad; badly; hardly; **nada mal** not bad; **dormi muito mal** I slept really badly; **mal se vê** you can hardly see it

mala suitcase; **fazer as malas** to pack

mal-educado/a rude

mal-entendido misunderstanding

mama breast

mamadeira baby's bottle

mancha stain; **mancha roxa** bruise

mandar to order; to send; **mandar vir** *(in restaurant)* to order; **mandar pelo correio** to post; **mandar revelar** to get developed

maneira way; **de qualquer maneira** anyway

manga sleeve

manhã morning

manter to keep

mão hand

mapa map

máquina machine; **máquina de lavar louça** dishwasher; **máquina de lavar roupa** washing machine; **máquina digital** digital camera; **máquina fotográfica** camera

mar sea

maravilha: ser uma maravilha to be lovely

marcar: marcar uma hora to make an appointment

marcha a ré reverse gear

março March

maré: maré alta high tide; **maré baixa** low tide

marido husband

marisco seafood

mas but

matar to kill

material material

mau/má bad; **mau tempo** bad weather

máximo/a maximum

me me; *(reflexive)* myself; **não me diga** don't tell me; **ele me conhece** he knows me; **me machuquei** I hurt myself

meados: em meados de setembro *(time)* in the middle of September

medicamento medicine, medication

médico/a doctor

médio/a medium; average

medo fear; **ter medo de** to be afraid of

meia-calça tights

meia-noite midnight

meia-pensão half-board

meias socks

meio/a half; middle; *(number on phone)* six; **no meio (de)** in the middle (of); **meio litro/quilo** half a litre/kilo; **em meio turno** part-time; **meia hora** half an hour; **meia volta** U-turn

meio-dia midday

mel honey

melhor best; better; **o/a melhor** the best; **é melhor ...** it's better to ...; **o meu melhor amigo** my best friend

melhorar to get better

membro member

menina girl

menino boy

menos less; least; **o/a menos** the least; **pelo menos** at least; **menos de** less than

mensagem message; text

menstruação period(s)

mentir to lie

mercado market

mercearia grocer's

mergulhar to dive

mergulho diving; **fazer mergulho** to go diving

mês month

mesa table

mesmo/a the same; **dá na mesma** it's all the same; **faço eu mesmo** I'll do it myself; **mesmo que** even if

metade half

metro metre

metrô underground

meu(s)/minha(s) my; mine; **um amigo meu** a friend of mine; **os meus/as minhas estão aqui** mine are here; **esse é o meu lugar** that's my seat

microondas microwave

mim me; **é para mim** it's for me

minha(s) see **meu(s)**

mínimo/a minimum

minuto minute

mirador viewpoint

missa mass

mobiliado/a furnished

mochila backpack, rucksack

mochileiro/a backpacker

moda fashion

modo way; **de qualquer modo** in any case

moderno/a modern

moeda coin; currency

moinho mill

molhado/a wet

momento moment; **neste momento** at the moment

montanha mountain

montar *(cavalgar)* to ride; *(organizar)* to set up

monte hill

monumento monument

mordida bite

morder to bite

morno/a lukewarm

morrer to die

morto/a dead

mosca fly

mosquito mosquito

mosteiro monastery

mostrar to show

moto motorbike

motor engine

motorista driver

motocicleta motorbike

mover to move; **mover-se** to move (oneself)

muçulmano/a muslim

mudança change

mudar to change; *(room, place)* to move; **mudar de roupa** to change (clothes)

mudo/a mute

muito(s)/muita(s) very; many; a lot; **muito contente** very happy; **muitas vezes** many times, often; **muitos deles** a lot of them

mulher woman

multa *(n)* fine

mundo world

muralha wall; rampart

muro *(external)* wall

músculo muscle

museu museum

música music

nacionalidade nationality
nada nothing; **de nada** not at all, you're welcome
nadar to swim
namorado/a boyfriend/girlfriend
não no; not; **não, obrigado/a** no, thank you; **não tenho idéia** no idea; **ainda não** not yet; **eu também não** neither do I; **não fumante** non-smoker
nariz nose
nascer to be born; **nasci em agosto** I was born in August
nascer do sol sunrise
natação swimming
Natal Christmas; **Feliz Natal!** Happy Christmas!
natureza nature
naturalidade place of birth
nécessaire toilet bag
necessário/a necessary
negativo (film) negative
negócios business; **a negócios** on business; **isso é um negócio meu** that's my business
negro/a black
nem neither; nor; **nem ... nem ...** neither ... nor ...; **nem eu** neither do I
nenhum(a) none; **não tenho idéia** I have no idea
nevar to snow
neve snow
nevoeiro fog
ninguém nobody
noite night; evening; **à noite** in the evening; **durante a noite** at nightime, during the night; **boa noite!** good night!
noiva fiancée
noivo fiancé
nome name; **em nome de** in the name of; **nome completo** full name; **nome (de batismo)** first name; **nome de família** family name
normal normal
norte north; **a norte de** (to the) north of; **no norte** in the north
nos us; (reflexive) ourselves; **ele nos conhece** he knows us
nós we

nosso(s)/a(s) ours; **um amigo nosso** a friend of ours; **são nossos/as** they are ours; **os nossos/as nossas estão aqui** ours are here
nota note; banknote
notícias news
novembro November
novo/a new; young; **de novo** again; **Ano Novo** New Year; **uma menina nova** a young girl
nu/nua naked
número number
número de telefone phone number
nunca never; **nunca mais** never again
nuvem cloud

o (pron) it, him; **os** them; **eu o/os conheço** I know him/them; **deixei-o no quarto** I left it in the room
o(s) (article) the
obra work; **em obras** under construction
obrigado/a thanks; **muito obrigado/a** thank you very much
obturação (in tooth) filling
ocasião occasion
oceano ocean
oculista optician
óculos glasses; **óculos de sol** sunglasses; **óculos de proteção** goggles
ocupado/a busy
ocupar to occupy; to take up; **ocupa muito espaço** it takes up a lot of space; **ocupar-se de** to deal with
oeste west; **a oeste de** (to the) west of; **no oeste** in the west
oferecer to offer
oficina garage
oi hi, hello
ok OK
olá hello, hi
óleo oil
olhar to look; **olhar para** to look at; to stare at
olho eye
ombro shoulder
onda wave
onde where; **onde é/são ...?** where is/are ...?; **de onde é?** where are you from?; **para onde vão?** where are you going?

ônibus bus; coach
ontem yesterday; **ontem à noite** yesterday evening
opaco/a matt
ópera opera
operar to operate
opinião opinion; **na minha opinião** in my opinion
oportunidade opportunity
ótimo/a great, wonderful; **ótimo!** great!
orelha ear
orelhão phone booth
orgânico/a organic
organizar to organize; to arrange; **organizar um encontro (com)** to arrange a meeting (with)
origem origin
orquestra orchestra
osso bone
ou or
ouro gold; **de ouro** gold, golden
outono autumn
outro(s)/outra(s) other; another; **outra vez** again; **os outros/as outras** the others
outubro October
ouvido ear
ouvir to hear; to listen
ovo egg

P

pacote packet
padaria bakery
padeiro baker
padre priest
pagar to pay
página page
pai father
pais parents
país country
paisagem landscape; scenery
palácio palace
palavra word
palavrão swearword
pálido/a pale
panela pot
pano cloth; fabric; **pano de chão** floor cloth; **pano de prato** tea towel
pão bread
papel paper; **papel higiênico** toilet paper
papelaria stationer's

par pair; **um par de sapatos** a pair of shoes
para for; **andar para a frente** to move forward
parabéns congratulations; **dar os parabéns a alguém** to congratulate someone
pára-brisa windscreen
pára-choque bumper
parada de ônibus bus stop
parar to stop; **sem parar** without stopping
parecer to seem; **parece que …** it seems that …; **parecer-se com** to look like; **o que lhe parece?** what do you think?
parque park; **parque de diversões** theme park
parte part; **dar parte de** to report; **fazer parte de** to be a part of
partida (n) departure; game; **partida de futebol** football match; **disputar uma partida de …** to have a game of …
partilhar to share
partir to leave; **a partir de segunda-feira** from Monday onwards
Páscoa Easter; **Feliz Páscoa!** Happy Easter!
passado (n) past
passado/a (adj) last; **no ano passado** last year
passageiro/a passenger
passagem ticket; way (through); **passagem só de ida** single (ticket); **passagem de ida e volta** return (ticket); **estar de passagem** to be passing through; **passagem de nível** level crossing; **passagem para pedestres** pedestrian crossing; **passagem subterrânea** subway; underpass
passaporte passport
passar to pass
passar a ferro to iron
pássaro bird
passe pass; season ticket
passear to stroll; **ir passear** to go for a stroll/a walk
passeio promenade; walk
pasta folder; briefcase
pasta de dentes tooth paste
pastilha para a garganta throat lozenge
paz peace; **deixe-me em paz!** leave me alone!
pé foot; **a pé** by foot
pedágio toll
pedestre pedestrian

peça piece; part; **peça de teatro** play; **peça sobressalente** spare part

pechincha bargain

pedaço bit; piece

pediatra paediatrician

pedido request; *(in restaurant)* order

pedir to ask; *(in restaurant)* to order; **pedir um favor** to ask a favour; **pedir emprestado/a** to borrow

pedra stone

pegar to catch; to pick up

peito chest

peixaria fishmonger's

peixe fish

pele skin

pêlo hair

pena pity; **é uma pena** it's a pity; **vale a pena** it's worth it

pensão guest house; **pensão completa** full board

pensar to think; **pensar em** to think about

pente comb

pequeno/a small, little

percurso route

perda loss

perdão forgiveness; **perdão?** pardon?

perder to lose; *(flight, train)* to miss; **perder-se** to get lost; **perder tempo** to waste time

perdido/a lost

perfume perfume

pergunta question

perguntar to ask; **fazer uma pergunta** to ask a question

perigoso/a dangerous

período period

perna leg

perto near, close by; **perto da praia** near the beach; **o/a mais perto** the nearest

pesado/a heavy

pescar to fish

pescoço neck

péssimo/a terrible

pessoa person

pia washbasin

piada joke

picada *(n)* bite; sting

picado/a stung; bitten; **ser picado/a (por)** to get stung (by); to be bitten (by)

picar to bite; to sting

pifar to break down

pijama pyjamas

pileque: estar de pileque to be drunk

pilha battery; pile

pílula do dia seguinte morning-after pill

pinça tweezers

pior worse; **é pior (do que)** it's worse (than); **o/a pior** the worst

piorar to get worse

piloto pilot; driver

piquenique picnic; **fazer um piquenique** to have a picnic

piscina swimming pool

pista track

pitoresco/a picturesque

placa plate; *(on road)* sign; **placa do carro** registration number

plano *(n)* plan

plano/a *(adj)* flat

planta plant

plástico plastic

pneu tyre

pó powder

pobre poor

poder to be able to; **não posso** I can't

pois as; well; therefore

polícia police; *(person)* policeman/policewoman

poluição pollution

pomada ointment

ponte bridge

ponto point; **duas horas em ponto** two o'clock sharp

por by; per; for; **feito por** made by; **por cento** percent; **por hora** per hour; **por dois dias** for two days

pôr to put; **pôr no correio** to post

pôr-do-sol sunset

por quê? why?

porque because

porta door

porta-malas *(car)* boot

portão gate; **portão de embarque** gate

portátil portable

porte postage

porto port; harbour

português/esa Portuguese

possível possible

postal postcard

pôster poster

posto de gasolina petrol station

posto de informações turísticas tourist office

pouco(s)/pouca(s) little; few; **pouco tempo** little time; **uns poucos** a few; **um pouco (de)** a bit (of); **... e pouco** (time) just after ...

poupar to save (money)

pousada guesthouse, bed and breakfast

praça square

praia beach

prancha de surfe surfboard

prata silver

prateado/a silver-plated

praticar to practise

prato plate; dish; **prato do dia** today's special; **prato principal** main dish

prazer pleasure; **muito prazer!** nice to meet you!

precisar de to need

preço price

preencher to fill in, to fill out

preferir to prefer

prêmio prize

preocupação worry

preocupar(-se) to worry; **não se preocupe** don't worry

preparar to prepare

presente present

preservativo condom

preso/a stuck

pressa hurry; **estar com pressa** to be in a hurry

pressão pressure; **pressão alta** high blood pressure; **pressão arterial** blood pressure; **pressão baixa** low blood pressure

prestes: estar prestes a to be about to

presunto ham

preto/a black; **em preto e branco** (film) black and white

prevenir to prevent; to warn

previsão do tempo weather forecast

primavera spring

primeiro/a first; **primeiro ...** first (of all) ...; **primeira classe** first class

primeiros-socorros first aid

principal main

principiante beginner

prioritário (mail) express

prisão prison; **prisão de ventre** constipation

privativo/a private

problema problem

procissão procession

procurar to look for; **procurar fazer** to try to do

produto product

professor(a) teacher

profissão profession

profundo/a deep

programa programme

progresso progress; **fazer progressos** to make progress

proibido/a forbidden

prometer to promise

promoção special offer

pronto/a ready; **estar pronto/a** to be ready

pronúncia accent

pronunciar to pronounce

propor to propose

propósito: de propósito on purpose

proprietário/a owner

próprio/a own; **o meu próprio carro** my own car

protetor solar sun cream

proteger to protect; **proteger-se (de)** to protect oneself (against)

protestante Protestant

provar (fact) to prove; (food) to try, to taste; (clothes) to try on

próximo/a next; close; **sou o próximo** I'm next; **próximo da janela** close to the window

publicidade publicity; advertising

público/a public

pulmão lung

pulseira bracelet

pulso wrist; pulse; **medir o pulso** to take one's pulse

puxar to pull

Q

quadra: quadra de tênis tennis court

quadrado/a square

quadril hip

quadro painting

qual/quais which; **o/a qual** which; **qual/quais?** which one/ones?

qualidade quality; **de boa/má qualidade** of good/poor quality

qualquer any; **qualquer coisa** anything; **qualquer um/pessoa** anyone

quando when

quanto how much; **quanto custa?** how much is it?; **quanto antes** as soon as possible; **há quanto tempo?** (for) how long?

quarta-feira Wednesday

quarto room; quarter; **quarto de hóspedes** guest room; **quarto duplo** double room; **quarto duplo com duas camas** twin room; **quarto individual** single room

quase almost

quatorze fourteen

que that; which; what; **o que é?** what is it?; **penso que** I think that

quê what?; **não tem de quê** not at all, don't mention it

quebrado/a broken; (phone) out of order

quebrar a perna to break one's leg

queijo cheese

queimadura burn; **queimadura do sol** sunburn

queimar to burn; **queimar-se** to burn oneself

queixar-se to complain

queixo chin

quem who; **quem fala?** who's calling?

quente warm; hot; **uma bebida quente** a hot drink

querer to want; **querer fazer alguma coisa** to want to do something; **querer dizer** to mean; **sem querer** unintentionally

querido/a dear

quilo kilo

quilômetro kilometre

quinta-feira Thursday

---

racista racist

radiador radiator

rádio radio

radiografia X-ray

rainha queen

raio ray; X-ray

rapar to shave

rápido/a fast, quick

raquete racket

raro/a rare; **raras vezes** seldom

rato mouse; rat

razoável reasonable

realidade reality

rebocar to tow

reboque breakdown truck; **a reboque** on tow

recado message

recarregar to recharge

receber to receive

receita recipe; (medical) prescription

recentemente recently

recepção reception

recepcionista receptionist

recibo receipt

reclamar to complain

recomendar to recommend

reconhecer to recognize

recordação souvenir; **como recordação** as a memento

recordar to remind; **recordar-se** to remember

recusar to refuse

redondo/a round

redução reduction

reduzir to reduce

reembolsar to refund; **ser reembolsado/a** to get a refund

reembolso refund

refeição meal

refúgio refuge

região region, area

regressar to come back; to return

regresso return

Reino Unido United Kingdom

religião religion

relógio clock; **relógio da luz** electricity meter; **relógio de pulso** watch

remetente sender

remédio medicine

reparação repair

reparar to repair; **mandar reparar alguma coisa** to get something repaired; **reparar em** to notice

repetir to repeat

reserva antecipada advance booking

reservado/a reserved

reservar to book, to reserve

resfriado cold

responder to answer

resposta answer

ressaca: estar de ressaca to have a hangover

restaurante restaurant

reto/a straight; **reto em frente** straight

ahead, straight on
retrato portrait
reumatismo rheumatism
reunião meeting
revelar to develop; **mandar revelar** *(photos)* to have developed
revista magazine
rico/a rich
rim kidney
rio river
rir to laugh
risco risk; line
rocha rock
rochedo cliff
roda wheel; **andar à roda** to turn; **roda sobressalente** spare wheel
rodízio set-price restaurant
rodoviária bus station
rollers rollerblades
rosa rose
rosto face
rotatória roundabout
roubalheira: é uma roubalheira it's a rip-off
roubar to steal
roubo theft
roupa clothes; **roupa de baixo** underwear; **roupa de mergulho** wetsuit
roupão bathrobe
rua street
ruim bad
ruínas ruins
ruivo/a *(hair)* red

S

sábado Saturday
sabão soap; **sabão em pó** washing powder
saber to know; **não sei nadar** I can't swim; **não sei** I don't know
sabonete soap
sabor flavour; taste
saca-rolhas corkscrew
sacar to withdraw *(money)*
saco bag; **saco de plástico** plastic bag; **saco de lixo** rubbish bag; **saco de dormir** sleeping bag
saia skirt
saída exit; way out; **saída de emergência** emergency exit
sair to come out/go out; to exit; **sair com**

alguém to go out with someone
sal salt
sala: sala de concertos concert hall; **sala de estar** living room
salgado/a salty
salto jump; *(of shoe)* heel; **usar salto alto** to wear high heels
salvar to save
sandálias sandals
sangrar to bleed
sangue blood
sanitários toilets
santo/a saint
sapato shoes
saque withdrawal *(money)*
satisfeito/a pleased
saudade: sentir/ter saudades de to miss
saúde health; **saúde!** bless you!
se *(pron)* itself; himself; herself; yourself; themselves; yourselves; **você se machucou?** did you hurt yourself?; **eles se machucaram** they hurt themselves; see *grammar*
se *(adv)* if; **se bem que** although; **se você não se importa** if you don't mind
seca drought
secador de cabelo hairdryer
secar to dry
seção section
seco/a dry
secretário/a secretary; **secretária eletrônica** answering machine
século century
seda silk
sede thirst; **ter/estar com sede** to be thirsty
segredo secret
seguir to follow
segunda-feira Monday
segundo/a second; **segunda classe** second class
segurança safety, security
segurar to hold; **segurar-se** to hold on
seguro *(n)* insurance
seguro/a *(adj)* safe; secure; sure
selecionar to select
selo stamp
sem without; **sem glúten** gluten-free
semáforo traffic lights
semana week; **durante a semana** during the week; **toda a semana** all week

sempre always; **sempre que** every time (that)

senão otherwise

senha password; PIN number

senhor Mr; sir; **o(s) senhor(es)** you

senhora Mrs; madam; **a(s) senhora(s)** you

senhoras ladies toilets

sensato sensible

sentar-se to sit down

sentido sense; direction

sentimento feeling

sentir to feel; **sentir-se bem/mal** to feel good/bad; **sentir-se mal** to feel sick; **sentir falta de** to miss

separado/a separate; separated

separar to separate; **separar-se** to split up

ser to be; **sou professora** I'm a teacher; **ser operado** to have an operation; **a não ser que** unless; **ou seja** in other words; **será que ...** I wonder if ...; **ser capaz de** to be able to; **é possível que chova** it might rain

sério/a serious

serviço service

servir to serve; *(clothes)* to fit; **servir para ...** to be good for ...; **servir-se de** to make use of

seta arrow

setembro September

seu(s)/sua(s) its; his; hers; your; yours; them; see *grammar*

sexo sex; gender

sexta-feira Friday

significar mean; **o que significa ...?** what does ... mean?

silêncio silence

silencioso/a silent

sim yes

simpático/a nice, friendly

simples simple

sinal sign; signal; **sinal de linha** ringtone; **sinal de trânsito** road sign

site website

situação situation

só only; alone; **só um** only one; **ele está só** he is alone

sobre about; over

sobremesa dessert

sobrenome surname

sociedade society

sócio member

socorro help; **pedir socorro** to ask for help

sofrer to suffer; **sofrer um acidente** to have an accident

sol sun; **ao sol** in the sun

solteiro/a single

som sound

sombra shade; **à sombra** in the shade

soneca nap; **tirar uma soneca** to have a nap

sonhar to dream

sonho dream

sono sleep; **ter sono** to be sleepy

sorrir to smile

sorriso smile

sorte luck; **boa sorte!** good luck!; **ter sorte** to be lucky

sotaque accent

Sr. Mr

Sra. Mrs; Miss; Ms

sua(s) see **seu(s)**

suar to sweat

suco juice

suficiente enough

sugerir to suggest

sujar-se to get dirty

sujo/a dirty

sul south; **a sul de** (to the) south of; **no sul** in the south

suor sweat

supermercado supermarket

suplemento supplement

suportar to stand; **não suporto isso** I can't stand it

surdo/a deaf

surfar to go surfing

surfe surfing

surpresa surprise

sustenido *(key)* hash

sutiã bra

T

tabacaria tobacconist's

tabaco tobacco

tabuleiro tray; board

taça bowl; cup; **uma taça de champagne** a glass of champagne

tal/tais such; **que tal?** what do you think?; how about it?; **tais como ...** such as ...

talão receipt; ticket; **talão de cheques** chequebook

talher cutlery

talvez maybe, perhaps

tamanho size

também also; **eu também não** me neither

tampa lid; *(of bottle)* top; *(of bathtub, sink)* plug

tampão para os ouvidos earplug

tanto(s)/a(s) so many; so much; **tanto melhor** all the better

tão so; **tão caro** so expensive

tapar to cover

tapete rug; mat; carpet

tarde *(n)* afternoon; **boa tarde!** good afternoon!

tarde *(adv)* late; **já é tarde** it's late; **chegar tarde** to arrive late

tarifa: tarifa normal full fare, full price; **tarifa reduzida** discount fare

taxa rate; duty; **taxa de câmbio** exchange rate

táxi taxi

taxista taxi driver

tchau bye

te you; yourself

teatro theatre

tecido fabric

tecla key

teclado keyboard

teleférico cable car

telefonar to phone, to telephone

telefone phone, telephone; **(telefone) celular** cell phone, mobile

telefonema phone call; **dar um telefonema** to make a phone call

telefonista switchboard operator

televisão television; **televisão a cabo** cable TV; **televisão por satélite** satellite TV

tem there is/there are

temperatura temperature; **medir/tirar a temperatura de alguém** to take someone's temperature

tempestade storm

templo temple

tempo weather; time; **o tempo está ruim** the weather's bad; **não tenho tempo para nada** I have no time for anything; **primeiro/segundo tempo** *(sport)* first/second half

temporal *(thunder)* storm

temporário/a temporary

tênis *(sport)* tennis; *(shoes)* trainers

tentar to try; **tentar fazer algo** to try to do

something

ter to have; **ter dor de cabeça** to have a headache; **tenho que ir** I have to go

terça-feira Tuesday

termômetro thermometer

terra earth; soil

terraço roof terrace

terramoto earthquake

térreo ground floor

terrível terrible

tesoura (pair of) scissors

testa forehead

teu(s)/tua(s) your; yours; **o teu bilhete está aqui** your ticket is here; **as tuas são estas** these are yours

tigela bowl

time team

tintim! cheers!

típico/a typical

tipo kind; type; **que tipo de ...?** what kind of ...?

tirar to take off/from/out; **tirar uma fotografia** to take a photo

toalete toilet

toalha towel; **toalha de banho** bath towel; **toalha de praia** beach towel; **toalha de rosto** hand towel

tocar to touch; *(instrument)* to play; **tocar à campainha** to ring the bell

todo/a whole; all; **o bolo todo** the whole cake; **todo o dia** all day; **toda gente** everybody; **ao todo** in total

todos/as every; everybody; **todos os dias** every day; **todas as semanas** every week; **todos foram** everybody went

tomada plug

tomar to take; **toma!** there you are!; **tomar banho de sol** to sunbathe

tonturas: sentir/ter tonturas to feel dizzy

topo top; **no topo** at the top

torcer to twist; **torcer o pé** to sprain an ankle; **torcer para** to support *(team)*

tornar-se to become

torneira tap

tornozelo ankle

torre tower

tosse cough; **ter tosse** to have a cough

tossir to cough

trabalhar to work

trabalho work

tradicional traditional
traduzir to translate
traje de banho swimming costume
tranqüilo/a peaceful; quiet
transferência transfer
transbordo: fazer transbordo to change *(trains etc)*
trânsito traffic
transpirar to sweat
transporte público public transport
trás: de trás back; **a porta de trás** the back door
travar to brake
trazer to bring
trem train
triste sad
trocador changing room
trocar to change, to exchange
troco change
trovoada thunderstorm
tu you
tua(s) see **teu(s)**
tubo pipe; tube
tudo all; **tudo incluído** all inclusive; **tudo bom?** how are things?
turismo tourism
turista *(n)* tourist
turístico/a *(adj)* tourist
turno turn; **em meio turno** part-time

U

último/a last
ultrapassar to overtake
um(a) a; one; **uma vez** once; **uma vez por dia/por hora** once a day/an hour
úmido/a humid
unha nail
urgência emergency
urgente urgent
usado/a used
usar to use; *(glasses, perfume)* to wear
usuário user
útil useful
utilizar to use
uva grape

V

vaca cow
vacinado/a (contra) vaccinated (against)

vagão carriage
vagão-leito sleeping car
vago vacant
vale valley; *(money)* voucher
valer to be worth; **vale a pena** it's worth it
validade validity
válido/a valid
valor value; amount
válvula stopcock
varanda balcony
vários/as several
vazio/a empty
vegetariano/a vegetarian
vela candle; *(car)* spark plug; *(sport)* sailing
velejar to sail
velho/a old
velocidade speed; **a toda a velocidade** at full speed
vencedor(a) winner
vendedor(a) shop assistant
vender to sell
vende-se for sale
venenoso/a poisonous
ventilador fan
vento wind
ventoinha fan
ventre belly
ver to see
verão summer
verdadeiro/a true
verde green; unripe
verdureiro greengrocer's
vime wicker
vergonha shame; embarassment
verificar to check
vermelho/a red
vertigem: ter vertigens to have vertigo
vespa wasp
véspera: na véspera the day before
vestiário changing room
vestido dress
vestir to wear; **vestir-se** to get dressed
vez turn; time; **muitas vezes** soften; **às vezes** sometimes, occasionally; **de vez em quando** from time to time; **três vezes ao dia** three times a day; **é a sua vez** it's your turn
via de acesso access road
viagem journey, trip; **boa viagem!** have a good trip!; **viagem de negócios** business trip

viajante traveller; passenger
viajar to travel
vida life
vídeo video
vidro glass
vigiar to watch (over)
vime wicker
violação rape; violation
vir to come; **venho de Porto Alegre** I come from Porto Alegre; **a semana que vem** next week
virar to turn; **virar-se** to get by; **virar à esquerda** to turn left
visita visit; tour; visitor; **visita guiada** guided tour
visitar to visit
vista view; eyesight; **até a vista!** see you!; **ter boa vista** to have a good eyesight
visto visa; **visto de entrada/saída** entry/exit visa
vitamina smoothie
vítima victim; casualty
vitrine shop window; **ver vitrines** to go window shopping
viúva widow
viúvo widower
viver to live
vivo/a alive
vizinho/a neighbour
voar to fly
você(s) you; yourself; yourselves; see *grammar*
volante steering wheel
voleibol, vôlei volleyball
volta turn; return; **dar a volta** to turn back; **estar de volta** to be back; **dar uma volta** to go for a walk/drive; **por volta de** *(time)* around; **na volta** on the way back
voltagem voltage
voltar to return; to turn
vomitar to vomit
vontade wish; **contra a vontade** against one's will; **de boa/má vontade** willingly/reluctantly; **ter vontade de** to want to do something
vôo flight
votos wishes; **votos de boas festas** seasons greetings; **votos de felicidades** best wishes
voz voice; **em voz alta/baixa** loudly/quietly

W

WC: WC das senhoras ladies' (toilet); **WC dos homens** gents' (toilet)
windsurfe windsurfing; **fazer windsurfe** to go windsurfing

X

xadrez chess
xale shawl
xampu shampoo
xarope syrup
xerox photocopy
xícara cup
xixi: fazer xixi to pee

Z

zangado/a angry
zero zero
zona area; **zona para pedestres** pedestrianized area

GRAMMAR

The definite and indefinite **articles** in Portuguese change according to gender and number, ie singular or plural noun:

	definite article (the)		indefinite article (a/an)	
	singular	plural	singular	plural
masculine	o	os	um	uns
feminine	a	as	uma	umas

The contractions with the definite article and the prepositions **a**, **de**, **em** and **por** are as follows:

a + o = ao	a + os = aos
a + a = à	a + as = às
de + o = do	de + os = dos
de + a = da	de + as = das
em + o = no	em + os = nos
em + a = na	em + as = nas
por + o = pelo	por + os = pelos
por + a = pela	por + as = pelas

The indefinite article can be contracted with the preposition **em**.

em + um = num   em + uma = numa

There are two **genders** in Portuguese. The majority of **nouns** ending in **o** are masculine, whereas most of those ending in **a** are feminine. The majority of nouns ending in **-ã**, **-gem**, **-ção**, **-ice** and **-ade** are feminine, eg:

o copo glass	a lã wool	a velhice old age
a casa house	a estação station	a cidade city
a mala suitcase	a garagem garage	

Words referring to people and their jobs can often be both masculine and feminine:

o/a gerente the manager	o/a doente the patient
o/a policial the policeman/policewoman	o/a guia the guide

Others change a final **o** to **a** or add an **a** to the final consonant:

médico → médica doctor   tradutor → tradutora translator

As a general rule, the plural of the noun is formed by adding an **s** at the end. However, the plural of nouns ending in **r**, **s** or **z** is formed by adding **es** to the end. Note that a few words already ending in **s** do not add another in the plural, eg ônibus, pires etc:

copo → copo**s**   casa → casa**s**
lugar → lugar**es**   nariz → nari**zes**
deus → deus**es**   ônibus → ônibus

The plural of nouns that end in **ão** can be formed in three different ways, the most common by far being **ões**:

balão → bal**ões**   canção → can**ções**
coração → cora**ções**   estação → esta**ções**

Some other words add **s**:

mão → mão**s**   cidadão → cidadão**s**

A few others add **ães**:

pão → p**ães**   cão → c**ães**

Nouns which end in **m** change it to **n** then add **s**:

garagem → garage**ns**   boletim → boleti**ns**
som → so**ns**   viagem → viage**ns**

Nouns which end in **l** change it to **i** then add **s** (note "e" and "o" before "i" acquire an acute accent):

hotel → hot**éis**   lençol → lenç**óis**
jornal → jorna**is**   barril → barr**is** (here just one **i** is written)

Nouns which end in **ês** form their plural in **eses**:

inglês → ingl**eses**   português → portugu**eses**.

Adjectives agree with the gender and number of the noun which they describe. They are usually placed after the noun:

a flor amarela the yellow flower   os limões amarelos the yellow lemons

Adjectives which end in **o** are placed in the feminine by replacing the **o** with an **a**. In general, adjectives which end in **ão** are placed in the feminine by replacing **ão** with **ã**. An **a** is added to the end of adjectives which end in **u** and **or**:

cru → cru**a**   acolhedor → acolhedor**a**

Adjectives which end in **ês** are placed in the feminine by replacing the **ês** with **esa**:

português → portugu**esa**   franc**ês** → franc**esa**

The plural of adjectives is formed in the same way as nouns.

Comparatives are used according to the formula **mais/menos ... do que ..., tão ... quanto ...**:

o hotel Itamari é **mais** confortável **do que** o hotel Embaixador
the hotel Itamari is more comfortable than the hotel Embaixador
a comida aqui é **tão** boa **quanto** a do outro hotel
the food here is as good as the food at the other hotel

As a rule, **superlatives** are formed by adding a definite article to the formula **mais/menos**:

o mais caro dos dois é o hotel Rio
the most expensive of the two is the hotel Rio
quais são **os mais** baratos?
which are the cheapest?

The following are some common adjectives with irregular comparatives and superlatives:

bom/boa good	**melhor** better	**o/a melhor** the best
grande big	**maior** bigger	**o/a maior** the biggest
mau/má bad	**pior** worse	**o/a pior** the worst

Demonstratives ("this"/"that") are used to show which people, animals or objects you are referring to. In Portuguese there are three forms: **este**, **esta**, **estes** and **estas** are used when the person or object is near to the speaker:

este homem this man

esse, **essa**, **esses** and **essas** are used when the object is nearer to the person you are speaking to (ie "that near you"):

gosto muito **desse** vestido I like that dress (ie the one you are wearing).

aquele, **aquela**, **aqueles** and **aquelas** are used when the person or object is further away (ie "that over there"):

vivo **naquela** casa lá I live in that house (over there).

There are also three neuter demonstratives meaning "this/that **thing**": **isto**, **isso** and **aquilo**:

isto é uma maçã this is an apple
isso é para amanhã that is for tomorrow
o que é **aquilo** lá em frente? what is that (over there) opposite?

Possessive adjectives

	masculine	feminine
my	**meu**	**minha**
your (de você)	**seu**	**sua**
his/her/its	**... dele/ dela**	**... dele/ dela**
our	**nosso**	**nossa**
your	**... de vocês**	**... de vocês**
their	**... deles/ delas**	**... deles/ delas**

Possessive pronouns

	masculine	feminine
mine	**o meu**	**a minha**
yours (de você)	**o seu**	**a sua**
his/hers/ its	**o dele/ dela**	**a dele/ dela**
ours	**o nosso**	**a nossa**
yours	**o de vocês**	**a de vocês**
theirs	**o deles/ delas**	**a deles/ delas**

Because of the ambiguity of **seu/sua**, it is much more usual to hear people say **o/a ... dele/dela/deles/delas** meaning "the ... of him/of her/of them". For example, instead of **a sua casa**, you will hear **a casa deles** their house (the house of them). We have simplified the table above so that **seu/sua** is always assumed to refer to "you" (**você**).

este é o meu lugar e o seu é aquele this is my seat and yours is that one

esse é o livro dela e o deles é este that is her book and theirs is this one

o quarto de vocês é maior do que o nosso your room is bigger than ours

In order to form the plural, you just need to add an **s**:

estes são os teus livros e esses são os meus these are your books and those are mine

Personal pronouns

Subject		Added to verb: Direct - Indirect			Reflexive		After preposition	
eu	I		**me**	me	**me**	myself	**mim**	me
você	you	**o/a** -	**lhe**	you	**se**	yourself	**você**	you
ele	he/it	**o** -	**lhe**	him/it	**se**	himself/itself	**ele**	him/it
ela	she/it	**a** -	**lhe**	her/it	**se**	herself/itself	**ela**	her/it
nós	we		**nos**	us	**nos**	ourselves	**nós**	us
vocês	you	**os/as** -	**lhes**	you	**se**	yourselves	**vocês**	you
eles	they	**os** -	**lhes**	them	**se**	themselves	**eles**	them
elas	they	**as** -	**lhes**	them	**se**	themselves	**elas**	them

Você is used generally for addressing people as "you"; **o senhor** and **a senhora** can be used in more formal situations. **Você**, **o senhor** and **a senhora** use the third person singular form of the verb.

 você é médico? are you a doctor?
 a senhora mora em Lisboa? do you live in Lisbon?

In the case of the **direct** object pronouns **o/a/os/as**, eg "him/her/them", colloquially you will find the subject pronouns used instead and **isso** used for "it":

 vimos **ela** na loja we saw her in the shop

In the case of the **indirect** object pronouns **lhe/lhes**, eg "to or for him/her/them", colloquially you will find **para** used with the forms normally used after a preposition see the right-hand column above.

 ela mostrou as fotografias **para eles** she showed them the photos

If the direct and indirect pronouns are both used together, the direct object is often omitted or **isso** used instead:

 vou dar (isso) para ele I am going to give it to him

More examples:

 desculpem, não vi **vocês** sorry, I didn't see you
 ele **me** deu o livro he gave me the book
 eles ainda não **lhe** telefonaram? haven't they phoned you yet?
 guardei **isso** para **você** I saved it for you

After certain prepositions, the personal pronoun contracts or adopts a special form:

em + ele/ela/eles/elas = **nele/nela/neles/nelas**
com + mim = **comigo**
com + nós = **conosco**

The **reflexive pronouns** are: **me**, **te**, **se**, **nos**, **vos**, **se** used according to the subject:

eu **me** vejo no espelho I see myself in the mirror
sirvam-**se**, por favor please help youselves

Personal subject pronouns can be dropped in Portuguese since the **verb** ending indicates who is doing the action:

almoço às 12.30   I eat at 12.30pm

Another form for "you", **tu**, still exists in certain parts of Brazil, especially in the south, but we have not included this form in the verb tables (apart from the present of the regular verbs shown below as an example) – in fact **tu** is often used colloquially with the same third-person verb form as **você**, so there is even less need to include it.

Portuguese **verbs** all end in either **-ar**, **-er** or **-ir** in the infinitive, apart from **pôr** "to put".

Regular verbs have the following endings in the present tense:

	andar	**comer**	**partir**
eu	and**o**	com**o**	part**o**
você	and**a**	com**e**	part**e**
ele/ela	and**a**	com**e**	part**e**
nós	and**amos**	com**emos**	part**imos**
vocês	and**am**	com**em**	part**em**
eles/elas	and**am**	com**em**	part**em**
tu	and**as**	com**es**	part**es**

The irregular verbs **ser** and **estar** both mean "to be". **Ser** indicates an inherent or permanent state, quality or characteristic and is used with occupations, nationalities and to tell the time and refer to permanent location. **Estar** normally indicates a non-permanent state, action or place.

está chovendo it's raining   estou em Recife I am in Recife
são nove horas it's nine o'clock   sou estudante I am a student
você é brasileiro? are you Brazilian?

Location is often expressed by using another verb meaning "to be", **ficar**:

onde fica o aeroporto? where is the airport?

As in other languages, irregular verbs are used very frequently in Portuguese and you should try to learn their forms separately as they do not follow a regular pattern.

The conjugation of **fazer** to make, **ir** to go, **pedir** to ask, **poder** to be able to, **querer** to want and **pôr** to put, will certainly be useful:

	eu	você	ele/ela	nós	vocês	eles/elas
ser	sou	é	é	somos	são	são
estar	estou	está	está	estamos	estão	estão
ter	tenho	tem	tem	temos	têm	têm
fazer	faço	faz	faz	fazemos	fazem	fazem
ir	vou	vai	vai	vamos	vão	vão
pedir	peço	pede	pede	pedimos	pedem	pedem
poder	posso	pode	pode	podemos	podem	podem
querer	quero	quer	quer	queremos	querem	querem
pôr	ponho	põe	põe	pomos	põem	põem

The **past simple** (or *preterite*) and the **past continuous** (or *imperfect*) are the most commonly used past forms. The first indicates that an action is completely finished, eg "I did something". The latter indicates an action which occurred over a period of time in the past, eg "I was doing something", and now may no longer do so, eg "I used to do something". Here are the conjugations for the regular verbs:

Past Simple (preterite)

	andar	comer	partir
eu	andei	comi	parti
você	andou	comeu	partiu
ele/ela	andou	comeu	partiu
nós	andamos	comemos	partimos
vocês	andaram	comeram	partiram
eles/elas	andaram	comeram	partiram

Past Continuous (imperfect)

	andar	comer	partir
eu	andava	comia	partia
você	andava	comia	partia
ele/ela	andava	comia	partia
nós	andávamos	comíamos	partíamos

	vocês	andavam	comiam	partiam
	eles/elas	andavam	comiam	partiam

... and of certain irregular verbs:

Past Simple

	eu	você	ele/ela	nós	vocês	eles/elas
ser	fui	foi	foi	fomos	foram	foram
estar	estive	esteve	esteve	estivemos	estiveram	estiveram
ter	tive	teve	teve	tivemos	tiveram	tiveram
fazer	fiz	fez	fez	fizemos	fizeram	fizeram
ir	fui	foi	foi	fomos	foram	foram
pedir	pedi	pediu	pediu	pedimos	pediram	pediram
poder	pude	pôde	pôde	pudemos	puderam	puderam
querer	quis	quis	quis	quisemos	quiseram	quiseram

Past Continuous

	eu	você	ele/ela	nós	vocês	eles/elas
ser	era	era	era	éramos	eram	eram
estar	estava	estava	estava	estávamos	estavam	estavam
ter	tinha	tinha	tinha	tínhamos	tinham	tinham
fazer	fazia	fazia	fazia	fazíamos	faziam	faziam
ir	ia	ia	ia	íamos	iam	iam
pedir	pedia	pedia	pedia	pedíamos	pediam	pediam
poder	podia	podia	podia	podíamos	podiam	podiam
querer	queria	queria	queria	queríamos	queriam	queriam

There is also a **future** tense which, as it indicates, expresses something that you "will/shall" do:

	andar	comer	partir
eu	andarei	comerei	partirei
você	andará	comerá	partirá
ele/ela/você	andará	comerá	partirá
nós	andaremos	comeremos	partiremos
vocês	andarão	comerão	partirão
eles/elas	andarão	comerão	partirão

The **conditional** tense indicates what you "would" do, should a certain situation occur:

	andar	comer	partir
eu	andaria	comeria	partiria
você	andaria	comeria	partiria
ele/ela	andaria	comeria	partiria
nós	andaríamos	comeríamos	partiríamos
vocês	andariam	comeriam	partiriam
eles/elas	andariam	comeriam	partiriam

To give a **command** (called the imperative), you use a special form of the verb called the subjunctive. This is formed by reversing the key vowel in the endings of verbs, ie the **a** of **-ar** verbs (**você anda**) changes to **e**, and the **e** of **-er** (**você come**) and **-ir** (**você parte**) verbs to an **a**:

fale com aquele senhor ali speak to that gentleman over there
não coma isso, está quente! don't eat it, it's hot!

Irregular verbs, as their name implies, are best learnt separately:

	você	**vocês**
ser	seja	sejam
estar	esteja	estejam
ter	tenha	tenham
fazer	faça	façam
ir	vá	vão
pedir	peça	peçam
dar	dê	dêem
querer	queira	queiram
pôr	ponha	ponham
vir	venha	venham

tenha cuidado – não o quebre be careful – don't break it
venha comigo come with me

In order to form the **negative** in Portuguese, it is sufficient to place **não** in front of the verb:

não conheço Lisboa I don't know Lisbon

Raising the tone of your voice towards the end of a sentence is sufficient to turn a statement from an affirmation into a **question**:

o quarto tem duas camas the room has two beds
o quarto tem duas camas? does the room have two beds?

HOLIDAYS AND FESTIVALS

BANK HOLIDAYS

Bank holidays are known as **feriados** and working days are called **dias úteis**. On bank holidays, administrative offices, banks and most shops are closed. The following is a list of Brazil's official holidays:

1 January	New Year's Day
February	Carnaval – Friday to Ash Wednesday
March/April	Good Friday
21 April	*Tiradentes* Day – celebrates the 1789 revolt against the Portuguese
1 May	Labour Day
May/June	Corpus Christi
7 September	Independence Day
12 October	*Nossa Senhora da Conceição Aparecida* – Patron Saint of Brazil
2 November	All Souls' Day
15 November	Proclamation of the Republic
25 December	Christmas Day

ANNUAL FESTIVALS AND EVENTS

Spring and autumn are probably the best times to experience local culture, although Brazil's fairly stable warm climate means that there are festivals all year round. Some important religious festivals are connected to the fact that Brazil has strong African roots and the cultures merged to produce a unique form of celebration. The following is a list of just some of the many festivals and events:

January

New Year's Day	Salvador – *Bom Jesus dos Navegantes* – a flotilla of boats accompanying the holy image crosses the bay to bring good luck for the New Year.
6th	In the north-east especially, Epiphany and the arrival of the Three Kings is an important religious festival.

February

2nd	*Dia de Nossa Senhora dos Navegantes* celebrated by

186

	both Catholics and Afro-Brazilians, the day of "Our Lady of the Sea" and *Iemanjá*, this is a holiday kept by most people who live beside the sea, rivers or lakes.
Carnaval	The world's largest party, as the whole of Brazil comes to a halt for five days – the best places to go are Rio de Janeiro, Salvador and Olinda.
March/April	Good Friday and Easter are widely celebrated, especially in Nova Jerusalém near Recife.
April 21st	*Tiradentes* Day – commemorates the execution of the national hero, Joaquim José da Silva Xavier, a rebel leader in the 1789 revolt against the Portuguese.
May	*Festa do Divino Espírito Santo* (Parati) – eight-day festival involving the crowning of an "Emperor", distributing food to the poor and sweets to children, processions, Masses, dancing and music.
June 24th	*Festa de São João* – mid-summer festival
June/July	Amazonian Cultural Festivals: festivals take place throughout June and July celebrating the culture of the Amazon: *Boi-Bumbá* (Ox-Dance); *quadrilhas caipiras* (African dancing); *pastorinhas* (medieval religious theatre). Last weekend in June: the oldest Ox-Dance festival takes place in Parintins, a competition between two dance groups (*Bois*) enacting a traditional folk tale. *Bumba Meu-Boi* São Luis, state capital of Maranhão – another festival dedicated to the Brazilian folk tradition of the ox. *Festas Juninas* Series of street festivals in late June/early July honouring Saint John, Saint Peter and Saint Anthony – bonfires, dancing and mock marriages. *Anima Mundi* Animation Festival held in Rio and São Paulo.

July	*Rio de Janeiro Pride* – Celebration of gay and lesbian pride in Rio de Janeiro.
August	São Paulo International Short Film Festival *Festa do Peão Boiadeiro* – the largest rodeo in the world in Barretos, plus Brazilian country music. *Festival de Cinema Brasileiro e Latino de Gramado* – Brazil's largest film festival, held in Gramado, Rio Grande do Sul.
September 7th 8th	 Independence Day parties and parades. *Festa de Nossa Senhora dos Remédios* (Parati) – celebrated in the old colonial town of Parati for 300 years. The patron saint is carried around the historic district. The cedarwood effigy is decorated with gold and silver earrings, chains and a crown and is kept under armed guard at the Parati Museum of Sacred Art.
mid-September	Rio de Janeiro International Book Fair *Festival do Rio* – important audiovisual event with numerous screenings and seminars at cinemas across the city.
October	*Oktoberfest* – Brazil has its own annual beer festival in Blumenau, where there are many descendents of German immigrants.
mid-October	*Círio de Nazaré* – Religious procession of Cirió in Belém on the second Sunday in October. Largest annual festival of the Amazon.
December New Year's Eve	 *Umbanda* Festival in Rio de Janeiro on Copacabana beach – millions of visitors, concerts, fireworks. African *Candomblé* worshippers dress in white to make offerings to the goddess of the sea *Iemanjá* – boats of flowers, jewellery and trinkets, with dancing by candlelight.

USEFUL ADDRESSES

IN THE UK
Embassy of Brazil
Tourist Office
32 Green Street
London W1K 7AT

Tel: 020 7629 6909
Fax: 020 7399 9102
E-mail: tourism@brazil.org.uk
Website: www.brazil.org.uk/

IN THE USA
Brazilian Embassy
3006 Massachusetts Avenue, NW
Washington, DC
20008-3634

Tel: (202) 238-2700
Fax: (202) 238-2827
Website: www.brasilemb.org/

IN BRAZIL
US Embassy
SES - Av. das Nações
Quadra 801, Lote 03
70403-900 - Brasilia, DF
Tel: (55) (61) 3312 7000
Fax: (55) (61) 3225 9136
Website: www.embaixadaamericana.org.br

British Consulate-General in Rio de Janeiro
Praia do Flamengo, 284/2°
22210-030
Rio de Janeiro RJ
Tel: (55) (21) 2555 9600
Fax: (55) (21) 2555 9671
E-mail: consular.rio@fco.gov.uk

(The British Consulate in Rio de Janeiro provides assistance in the following states: Rio de Janeiro, Espírito Santo, Minas Gerais, Bahia, Sergipe, Alagoas, Pernambuco, Paraíba, Rio Grande do Norte, Ceará, Piauí, Maranhão.)

British Consulate-General in São Paulo
Rua Ferreira de Araujo, 741 – 2 andar
Pinheiros
Sao Paulo – SP
05428-002
Tel: (55) (11) 3094 2700
Fax: (55) (11) 3094 2717
Email: saopaulo@gra-bretanha.org.br
Website: www.uk.org.br

(The British Consulate in São Paulo provides assistance in the following
states: São Paulo, Mato Grosso do Sul, Paraná, Santa Catarina, Rio Grande
do Sul).

Directory enquiries: 102
Emergency numbers: 190 – Police; 192 – Ambulance; 193 – Fire.
Airport information: www.infraero.gov.br
Camping: www.campingclube.com.br
Youth hostels: www.hostel.org.br
News in English: www.brazilpost.com
Official Brazilian tourist site: www.turismo.gov.br
São Paulo city website: http://anhembi.terra.com.br/turismo/eng/
Rio de Janeiro Convention and Visitors Bureau:
www.rioconventionbureau.com.br
RIOTUR – City of Rio de Janeiro Tourism Authority
Rua da Assembléia, 10 – 9º andar
Centro Cep 20011–901
Rio de Janeiro – RJ
Tel.: (21) 2217 7575
E-mail: riotur.riotur@pcrj.rj.gov.br
Website: www.rio.rj.gov.br/riotur/en/

CONVERSION TABLES

Note that when writing numbers, Portuguese uses a comma where English uses a full stop. For example 0.6 would be written 0,6 in Portuguese, and 1,500 would be written 1.500.

Measurements
For everyday measurements the metric system is used in Brazil.

Length
1 cm ≈ 0.4 inches
30 cm ≈ 1 foot

Distance
1 metre ≈ 1 yard
1 km ≈ 0.6 miles

To convert kilometres into miles, divide by 8 and then multiply by 5.

kilometres	1	2	5	10	20	100
miles	0.6	1.25	3.1	6.25	12.50	62.5

To convert miles into kilometres, divide by 5 and then multiply by 8.

miles	1	2	5	10	20	100
kilometres	1.6	3.2	8	16	32	160

Weight
25g ≈ 1 oz   1 kg ≈ 2 lb   6 kg ≈ 1 stone

To convert kilos into pounds, divide by 5 and then multiply by 11.
To convert pounds into kilos, multiply by 5 and then divide by 11.

kilos	1	2	10	20	60	80
pounds	2.2	4.4	22	44	132	176

Liquid
1 litre ≈ 2 pints
4.5 litres ≈ 1 gallon

Temperature
To convert temperatures in Fahrenheit into Celsius, subtract 32, multiply by 5 and then divide by 9.
To convert temperatures in Celsius into Fahrenheit, divide by 5, multiply by 9 and then add 32.

Fahrenheit (°F)	32	40	50	59	68	86	100
Celsius (°C)	0	4	10	15	20	30	38

Clothes sizes

In Brazil, you'll find sizes using the following abbreviations **RN** (new born), **P** (Small), **M** (Medium), **G** (Large) and **GG** (Extra Large), but the English-language abbreviations, **XS** (Extra Small), **S** (Small), **M** (Medium), **L** (Large) and **XL** (Extra Large) are also used.

Note also that the sizes on this page can only be a very rough guide owing to the different ways that manufacturers size and label their garments, even in the same country!

• Women's clothes

UK	6	8	10	12	14	16	etc
US	4	6	8	10	12	14	
BR	38	40	42	44	46	48	

• Bras: basically the same, although cup sizes may vary

• Men's shirts (collar size)

UK	14	15	16	17	etc
BR/US	35	38	41	43	

• Men's clothes

UK	30	32	34	36	38	etc
US	40	42	44	46	48	
BR	50	52	54	56	58	

Shoe sizes
• Women's shoes

UK	4	5	6	7	8	etc
US	6	7	8	9	10	
BR	35	36	37	38	39	

• Men's shoes

UK	7	8	9	10	11
US	8	9	10	11	12
BR	39/40	40/41	41/42	42/43	43/44